The ESSENTIALS of

Income
Taxation

Mark A. Segal, J.D., LL.M., CPA
Assistant Professor of Accounting
University of South Alabama, Mobile, AL

William D. Keller, Ed.D.
Professor Emeritus of Accounting
Ferris State University, Big Rapids, MI

Research & Education Association
61 Ethel Road West
Piscataway, New Jersey 08854

THE ESSENTIALS®
OF INCOME TAXATION

Printed in the United States of America

Library of Congress Catalog Card Number 00-130643

International Standard Book Number 0-87891-880-9

WHAT "THE ESSENTIALS" WILL DO FOR YOU

This book is a review and study guide. It is comprehensive and it is concise.

It helps in preparing for exams and in doing homework, and remains a handy reference source at all times.

It condenses the vast amount of detail characteristic of the subject matter and summarizes the **essentials** of the field.

It will thus save hours of study and preparation time.

The book provides quick access to the important principles, concepts, formulas, and laws in the field.

Materials needed for exams can be reviewed in summary form— eliminating the need to read and re-read many pages of textbook and class notes. The summaries will even tend to bring detail to mind that had been previously read or noted.

This "ESSENTIALS" book has been prepared by experts in the field, and has been carefully reviewed to ensure accuracy and maximum usefulness.

Dr. Max Fogiel
Program Director

CONTENTS

CHAPTER 1

BASIC PRINCIPLES

1.1 What is a Tax?

A tax is a measure primarily imposed to raise revenue so that the government can meet its responsibility to provide for the general welfare and defense of its citizens as well as pay its debts.

1.2 Other Functions of Federal Taxation

Our tax system is influenced by several objectives in addition to the raising of revenue for the government. These other objectives include:

1) **Economic Considerations**—motivating investment behavior and employment.

2) **Social Considerations**—motivating charitable giving and helping out the poor.

3) **Equity**—being fair to all taxpayers.

4) **Political Considerations**—the lobbying of special interest groups and political compromise.

1.3 Sources of the Tax Law

Article 16 of the Constitution provides Congress with the power to lay and collect income taxes. There exist several sources of authority for determining the tax law on an issue. These include:

1) **The Internal Revenue Code (IRC)**—Except for violation of the Constitution the provisions of the Internal Revenue Code are binding on all courts. While the Internal Revenue Code is the primary source of the tax law, often other sources must be resorted to in order to see how an I.R.C. provision applies.

2) **Legislative History**—The legislative history is composed of the published reports of legislative committees concerning the I.R.C. provision in question.

3) **Regulations**—Regulations are the interpretation and explanation of the I.R.C. provision by the Treasury Department. Although interpretive, the regulations are given significant weight by the courts.

4) **Revenue Rulings**—These are official pronouncements of the IRS National Office which indicate the way the IRS would treat a given situation for tax purposes.

5) **Letter Rulings**—Individual rulings issued to taxpayers upon request indicating the tax treatment of a fact situation described by the taxpayer. A letter ruling is only binding on the Service with regard to the taxpayer and fact situation upon which it is issued.

6) **Court Decisions**—The trial courts for tax purposes are the Tax Court, Federal District Court, and Claims Court. Appeals from the trial court decisions are taken to the appropriate U.S. Court of Appeals. Cases of the U.S. Court of Appeals may be reviewed, but only upon the granting of a writ of certiorari by the U.S. Supreme Court. The Supreme Court decisions on a matter control the decisions of lower courts.

1.4 Role of the IRS

The IRS is the agency within the Treasury Department which is responsible for the enforcement of the Federal tax law.

1.5 How a Tax Bill Becomes Law

Tax bills originate in the House of Representatives where the bill must be reviewed by the House Ways and Means Committee.

If the bill is approved by the House Ways and Means Committee, it is then brought before the full House. If the bill is approved by the House, it is then referred to the Senate Finance Committee.

The Senate Finance Committee holds hearings on the bill, after which a report is made to, and the bill heard by the full Senate, at which time Senators have the opportunity to offer an amendment to the bill.

If there is no discrepancy between the House and Senate versions of the bill, it is then referred to the president who will sign the bill into law or veto it. Should the president veto the bill, it may still become law if the veto is overridden by a sufficient vote of both houses of Congress.

If a discrepancy exists between the House and Senate versions of the bill, a joint conference committee is formed to work out a compromise bill. If the compromise bill is approved by the House and Senate, it is then sent to the president who will sign it into law or veto it. Should the president veto the bill, it will still be made law if the veto is overridden by Congress.

1.6 Steps in Computing Individual Income Tax

Step 1—Determine Total Gross Income

Gross income includes all income regardless of its source unless there is an express exclusion from tax. Cases have clarified the definition of gross income. In general, an item of gross income is typically characterized by an increase in the taxpayer's net worth, attributable to labor or capital, involving the receipt of property not held previously. Examples of inclusions in gross income include wages, salary, dividends, and rents. Mere increases in the value of an asset held or loan proceeds received do not constitute gross income. Interest on municipal bonds, and receipts of gifts and inheritances do not constitute gross income for income tax purposes either.

Step 2—Subtract Deductions toward Adjusted Gross Income from Gross Income

Deductions toward adjusted gross income are a special category of deductions. Major deductions falling into this category include alimony payments, losses on dispositions of property, and most expenses incurred in one's self-employment or rental activities. The adjusted gross income figure is particularly important in that certain deductions and credits are affected by the taxpayer's adjusted gross income.

Step 3—Subtract the Greater of the Taxpayer's Standard Deduction Amount or Total Allowable Itemized Deductions from Adjusted Gross Income

Itemized deductions include allowable deductions expenses typically more personal in nature, e.g., medical expenses, home mortgage interest, moving expenses, and charitable contributions, as well as most employee business expenses. The taxpayer's standard deduction meanwhile is dependent upon the taxpayer's filing status. A taxpayer's standard deduction amount will be adjusted upward should the taxpayer be elderly (65 or older for tax purposes) and/or blind.

Step 4—Subtract the Total Exemption Amount for the Year from the Subtotal of Steps 1–3 to Determine Taxable Income

The exemption amount equals the total number of exemptions claimed by the taxpayer multiplied by the amount allowed by the federal government per exemption for the year.

Step 5—Compute the Taxpayer's Tax Liability by Use of Tax Tables or Rate Schedules Provided by the IRS

If the taxable income is less than $50,000, the taxpayer may choose to use either the tax tables or the tax rate schedule that fits the taxpayer's status. Should the taxable income be $50,000 or more, the tax rate schedules issued by the Service must be used.

Step 6—Determine the Amount of Tax that Must be Paid or the Credit Against Future Taxes or Refund to which the Taxpayer is Entitled

Subtract the estimated taxes paid, taxes withheld from wages, and credits from the taxpayer's tax liability.

1.7 Tax Schematic

Gross Income
— Deductions Toward Adjusted Gross Income
Adjusted Gross Income
— The Greater of the Taxpayer's Standard Deduction Amount or Total Allowable Itemized Deductions
Subtotal
— Total Exemption Amount
Taxable Income
Use Taxable Income to Compute Tax Liability
Tax Liability
— Estimated Taxes Paid, Federal Income Tax Withheld, and Credits
Payments Owed or Refund or Credit to which Entitled

Review Questions

1. *What is a tax?*

   A tax is primarily a measure to raise revenue for the government to enable its providing for the general welfare and defense as well as pay its debts.

2. *What article of the Constitution authorizes Congress to lay and collect income taxes?*

   Article 16 of the Constitution equips Congress with the power to lay and collect income taxes.

3. *What are the major types of tax authority?*

   There exists a wide array of tax authority. These include the Constitution, Internal Revenue Code, legislative history, regulations, revenue rulings, letter rulings, and court decisions. Of these the Constitution, Internal Revenue Code, and Supreme Court decisions are the most authoritative.

4. *What are the trial courts for tax purposes?*

   The trial courts for tax purposes are the Tax Court, the Federal District Court, and the U.S. Claims Court.

5. *What courts may the tax trial court decisions be appealed to?*

   The tax trial court decisions may be appealed to the appropriate U.S. Court of Appeals. U.S. Court of Appeals decisions may in turn be reviewed by the U.S. Supreme Court but only upon granting a writ of certiorari.

6. *What is the function of the IRS?*

   The IRS is responsible for the enforcement of the Federal tax law.

7. *Where does a Federal tax bill originate?*

Federal tax bills originate in the House of Representatives, where they must be reviewed by the House Ways and Means Committee.

8. *What is a joint conference committee?*

A joint conference committee is a committee formed when the House and Senate version of a tax bill differ. The committee's function is to work out a mutually agreeable bill.

9. *What are the steps in computing an individual's Federal income tax?*

The steps involved in computing an individual's Federal income tax involve: a) Calculating the taxpayer's gross income and subtracting therefrom the taxpayer's deductions toward adjusted gross income, the greater of the taxpayer's standard deduction amount or itemized deductions, and total exemption amount to derive taxable income. b) The taxable income figure is then used to determine the taxpayer's tax liability. The tax liability is then reduced by credits, estimated income taxes paid and Federal income taxes withheld to derive the amount of tax owed by the taxpayer or the refund or credit to which the taxpayer is entitled.

10. *Which is preferable, deductions toward adjusted gross income or itemized deductions?*

Deductions toward adjusted gross income are preferable to itemized deductions because: a) all taxpayers can benefit from deductions toward adjusted gross income, while only itemizers can benefit from itemized deductions; and b) even if one itemizes, itemized deductions only provide a partial tax benefit as had the taxpayer not itemized he would have been entitled to at least the standard deduction anyway.

11. *Which are preferable, deductions or credits?*

Credits are preferable because a dollar of credit will offset a dollar of tax liability; whereas a dollar of deduction only produces a tax savings equal to the dollar multiplied by the taxpayer's marginal tax rate.

CHAPTER 2

FILING STATUS AND EXEMPTIONS

2.1 The Importance of Filing Status

Determining a taxpayer's filing status is one of the most significant decisions that must be made for tax purposes. Filing status affects:

1) Whether the taxpayer must file a return.

2) Whether the taxpayer will use the standard deduction or itemized deductions.

3) The tax rate to which the taxpayer will be subject.

4) Limitations that might apply to deductions and credits of the taxpayer.

2.2 Types of Filing Status

Married Filing Jointly—is generally the most desirable filing status due to a preferable standard deduction amount and tax rate structure. Taxpayers qualify to file a joint return if they meet any of the following on the last day of the taxable year:

1) Were married and living as husband and wife.

2) Were living in a common-law marriage as recognized by the state within which the taxpayer lives.

3) Could file, for the year a spouse dies, a joint return for the surviving spouse, and decedent, if the surviving spouse during the year has not remarried, and if the surviving spouse was entitled to file a joint return when the decedent died.

4) Were separated but not under a judicial decree of divorce or separate maintenance.

5) Were separated under an interlocutory (not final) decree of divorce.

6) Were electing, if married to a nonresident alien, to report all of the alien spouse's worldwide income.

Qualified Surviving Spouse—For up to two years after the year one's spouse dies, joint return rates may be used by the surviving spouse if the surviving spouse has not remarried and:

1) is a citizen or resident of the United States.

2) can qualify to file a joint return for the year his or her spouse died.

3) has a dependent child who can be claimed as a dependent, who lives with such spouse and with regard to whom the spouse pays more then 1/2 of the cost of maintaining the household where the spouse and child live.

Abandoned Spouse—Although technically married, a spouse will be considered unmarried for tax purposes if the spouse:

1) does not file a joint return.

2) pays more than 1/2 of the cost of maintaining the household.

3) has lived apart from his or her spouse for at least the last six months of the taxable year.

4) has the home be the principal residence of a child, who can be claimed as a dependent (unless such is waived) for more than 1/2 of the taxable year.

Married Filing Separately—Taxpayers who are married but do not qualify for joint return status or do not consent to the filing of a joint return may file as married filing separately.

Head of Household—Generally viewed as the status most desirable tax-wise next to married filing jointly. To file as head of household, the taxpayer:

1) must be considered unmarried for tax purposes at the end of the taxable year.

2) must have a household which is the principal residence of at least one relative.

3) must pay over 1/2 of the cost of maintaining the household.

4) cannot be a nonresident alien.

Note that parents for whom over 50% of the cost of where they reside is provided by the taxpayer need not live in the taxpayer's household.

Single—Any taxpayer who is not considered married for tax purposes is eligible to file a single return.

2.3 Who Must File a Return

As a general rule a taxpayer must file a tax return if the taxpayer's gross income exceeds the taxpayer's regular standard deduction amount (based upon the taxpayer's filing status) plus an adjustment for old age if applicable plus the taxpayer's total personal exemption amount that can be claimed for the year.

Exceptions

Certain taxpayers must file a tax return if they have gross income greater than the taxpayer's personal exemption amount for the year. This rule pertains to taxpayers married filing separately, nonresident aliens, and U.S. citizens entitled to exclude income from U.S. possessions.

Special Rules

Special rules govern whether taxpayers who are self-employed or who can be claimed as a dependent by another must file.

2.4 Personal Exemptions

The amount per exemption is subject to an annual cost of living adjustment. Taxpayers can typically claim a personal exemption for themselves on their own return. No personal exemption is permitted, however, to a taxpayer who can be claimed as a dependent by another.

Joint Returns

In the case of a joint return two personal exemptions can usually be claimed—one for the husband and one for the wife.

2.5 Dependency Exemptions

In order to claim a person as your dependent, five tests must be satisfied:

1) **Support Test**—The taxpayer must provide more than 50% of the dependent's support. In determining whether this standard is met, the cost of such items as medical care, food, education, and value of lodging are considered, and any scholarships received by the dependent are ignored.

   Exceptions—The support test need not be satisfied:

   a) with regard to a child if the taxpayer is divorced or separated from the custodial spouse.

   b) where the taxpayer has the right to claim the dependency exemption pursuant to a valid multiple support agreement.

2) **Gross Income Test**—The dependent's gross income must be less than the exemption amount for the taxable year.

Exceptions—The gross income test need not be satisfied when the dependent is a child of the taxpayer and either under the age of 19 or a full-time student under the age of 24.

EXAMPLE

Taxpayer's child is 18 years of age and has gross income for the year exceeding the amount per exemption. The child's gross income will not cause failure of the gross income test, due to the child being under 19 and the child of the taxpayer.

3) **Relationship Test**—The dependent must either be related to the taxpayer in a certain prescribed manner, or be a member of the taxpayer's household the entire taxable year.

   Note that foster children and cousins of the taxpayer are not considered sufficiently related. Perhaps surprisingly, however, in-laws of the taxpayer continue to be sufficiently related even though the marriage giving rise to their in-law status has terminated.

4) **Joint-Return Test**—A dependency exemption cannot be claimed for someone who has filed a joint return, unless the filing of such joint return was not required and was only done to obtain a tax refund.

5) **Citizenship or Resident Test**—The dependent must have been a citizen or resident of the United States, Canada, or Mexico during some part of the taxable year.

2.6 Types of Returns

There exist three basic types of tax returns: the 1040, also known as the long form, and the 1040A and 1040EZ, which are referred to as short forms. Severe restrictions are placed upon taxpayer's ability to utilize the 1040A and 1040EZ.

2.7 Filing

Individual taxpayers are required to file their tax return by the 15th day of the 4th month following the end of their taxable year. This generally results in an April 15 due date. Should such 15th day fall on a Saturday, Sunday, or legal holiday the return will be due the first business day thereafter.

EXAMPLE

John is a taxpayer whose tax year runs from January 1 to December 31. If April 15 (the 15th day of the 4th month following the end of John's taxable year) falls on a Saturday, John's return due date will be Monday, April 17.

2.8 Extensions

Taxpayers filing a 1040 or 1040A can obtain an automatic four-month extension of filing by filing a Form 4868 by the regular return-due date. An additional two-month extension may later be applied for through the filing of a form 2688, but receipt of such additional extension is within the discretion of the Service.

Review Questions

1. *What are the types of filing status?*

    The types of filing status for individual taxpayers are: married filing jointly, qualified surviving spouse, head of household, single, and married filing separately.

2. *Which filing status is generally the most desirable?*

    Married filing joint is generally the most desirable status due to a preferable rate structure, higher standard deduction, and more advantageous ceilings and floors on certain deductions and credits.

3. *If a taxpayer is married, and his/her spouse does not consent to the filing of a joint return, must married filing separately status be used if a return is required to be filed?*

Married filing separately status may still be avoided in this circumstance if the taxpayer qualifies as an abandoned spouse. If an abandoned spouse, the taxpayer will be considered unmarried for tax purposes.

4. *What is the general rule for determining if a tax return must be filed?*

Under the general rule a return must be filed if the taxpayer's gross income exceeds the taxpayer's regular standard deduction amount (adjusted for old age if applicable) plus total personal exemption amount.

5. *What are the two types of exemptions?*

The two types of exemptions are the personal exemption and dependency exemption.

6. *What tests must be satisfied in order to claim someone as your dependent?*

There are five basic tests which must be satisfied (or an exception for which a test qualified). These are:

1) the gross income test

2) the support test

3) the relationship test

4) the joint return test

5) the citizenship or residency test

7. *What are the types of individual tax returns?*

The types of individual tax returns are the Forms 1040A and 1040EZ (referred to as the short form) and the 1040 (referred to as the long form).

8. *What is the regular return due date?*

   The regular return due date for an individual tax return is the 15th day of the fourth month following the end of the taxable year, unless such day falls on a Saturday, Sunday, or legal holiday in which case the first business day thereafter is the regular return due date.

9. *How may an automatic four-month extension be acquired?*

   An automatic four-month extension on filing can be acquired with regard to a 1040A or 1040 by filing a Form 4868 by the regular return due date. However, this does not postpone payment.

CHAPTER 3

EXCLUSIONS FROM GROSS INCOME

3.1 Definition of Exclusions

An exclusion is an item not included in gross income. An item may be excludable from gross income due to:

1) not meeting the criteria of gross income;

2) being nontaxable under the U.S. Constitution; or

3) being excludable under a provision of the tax law (the Internal Revenue Code).

3.2 Gifts and Inheritance

An item received as a gift or inheritance is excludable from the recipient's gross income. Income on the property so received will generally be taxable. To determine if amounts received are taxable the nature of such amounts must be determined. Thus, for example, interest on an inherited bank account is taxable whereas interest on an inherited municipal bond is not.

3.3 Scholarships

Under current law a scholarship will be excludable only if the recipient is a degree-seeking candidate. If a degree-seeking candidate, the exclusion is allowed, but only for:

a)   tuition and fees for attending a qualified institution

b)   fees, books, supplies, and other course-related amounts

Amounts received labelled scholarship which are received for teaching or research will generally be includable in the recipient's gross income.

3.4 Damages

The tax treatment of damages depends upon the classification of the damages:

1)   Damages received for personal injuries as well as slander and libel are excluded from gross income.

2)   Damages received characterized as punitive damages are generally includable in gross income. Such damages are only excludable from gross income if associated with personal injuries.

3)   Damages received for property damages are excludable from gross income up to the amount of the taxpayer's basis in the asset.

3.5 Life Insurance

Life insurance constitutes one of the most significant assets with which most of us have to deal. When an individual takes out a life insurance policy on his (her) own life and dies, payment of the proceeds in a lump sum to the beneficiary (beneficiaries) will be excludable from the beneficiary's (beneficiaries') gross income. When the policy is instead paid out in installments, the portion of each payment representing interest will be includable in the recipient's gross income.

EXAMPLE

J has a life insurance policy covering his life with a face amount of $100,000 of which his daughter is the sole beneficiary. Upon J's death the daughter decides to receive the proceeds on an installment basis. She is to receive the proceeds in 10 equal annual installments. In year 1 she receives a payment of $11,000. Of this amount $10,000 is excluded from gross income ($100,000 divided by 10) and $1,000 is included in gross income.

It should be noted that when the beneficiary is the decedent's surviving spouse and the decedent died before October 22, 1986, the surviving spouse is entitled to an additional exclusion of up to $1,000 per year.

3.5.1 Dividends

Dividends are often paid on life insurance policies. Such dividends are excludable from gross income of the policyholder until the aggregate of the dividends received exceeds the aggregate of the premiums paid on the policy.

3.5.2 Surrender of the Policy

If the policy is returned to the insurance company for cash surrender value, should the cash surrender value received exceed the policyholder's investment in the policy, such excess must be included in the policyholder's gross income. Should the cash surrender value be less, however, than the investment in the policy no deduction is permitted.

3.5.3 Sale of Policy

If a policy is sold by the insured, the insured must include in gross income any excess of the amount received over the insured's investment in the policy. Typically where the policy is sold, the purchaser will have an inclusion in gross income when the insured dies equal to the difference between the face amount of the policy and the purchaser's investment in the policy.

3.6 Special Insurance Plans and Benefits

Group Term Life Insurance—Premiums paid by an employer on behalf of an employee for coverage of up to $50,000 are excludable from the employee's gross income.

Accident and Health Insurance—Reimbursements for medical care costs from an accident and health plan are generally excludable from gross income. If you paid the entire premium for your medical insurance, you do not include an excess reimbursement in your gross income. If your employer pays the total cost of your medical insurance plan and your employer's contributions are not included in your income, you must report all excess reimbursements as income. If both you and your employer contribute to your medical insurance plan and your employer's contributions are not included in your income, include in your income the part of an excess reimbursement that is from your employer's contributions.

Workmen's Compensation—Workmen's Compensation recoveries are excluded from gross income.

Disability Policies—Amounts received from disability policies paid for by an employee are excludable from the employee's gross income.

3.7 Social Security Benefits

A portion of Social Security benefits received must be included in gross income if an excess is produced by the formula shown on the following page.

If the formula produces an excess, the taxpayer must include in gross income the lesser of 50% of the excess or 50% of the Social Security benefits received.

3.8 Employee Fringe Benefits

The tax law excludes numerous employee fringe benefits from gross income. Such excluded benefits include:

SOCIAL SECURITY BENEFITS WORKSHEET FORMULA

1. 50% of social security benefits received for the year
2. Plus *Modified Adjusted Gross Income* (wages, salaries, taxable and nontaxable interest income, dividend income, taxable refunds of state and local taxes, alimony received, business income or loss, capital gain or loss, capital gain distributions, other gains or losses, pensions, annuities, rent and royalty and partnership and estate and trust income, farm income or loss, and unemployment compensation) less adjustments to income (IRA and Keogh deductions, early withdrawal penalties, alimony paid)
3. Less Base Amount
   a. $25,000 for singles and heads of household and qualifying widow(er) with dependant child
   b. $32,000 for a married couple filing a joint return
   c. 0 for married filing separately
4. Equal the excess

Again, if the formula produces an excess, the taxpayer must include in gross income the lesser of 50% of the excess or 50% of the social security benefits received.

1) **De Minimis Fringe Benefits**—These are benefits considered so small in dollar amount that it is impractical to require their inclusion in gross income, e.g., coffee, donuts, use of company secretarial services, photocopier, and supplies.

2) **No Additional Cost Fringe Benefits**—To qualify for this exclusion the benefit must be received in the same line of business as that in which the employee works and not produce a substantial additional cost to the employer. For example, the ability of an airline employee to enjoy a free trip on the employer's airline but only on a standby basis.

3) **Qualified Employee Discounts**—An employee is permitted to exclude from gross income: A discount of up to 20%

of the cost charged to customers for services of the employer, and an amount not in excess of the gross profit percentage for property bought from the employer, e.g., inventory.

3.9 Tax Exempt Interest

Interest on state, municipal, and political subdivision bonds or obligations are generally excludable from gross income.

3.10 Annuities

An annuity is the right to periodic payments for a fixed period. Generally, an annuity covers either a term of years or the taxpayer's lifetime. In general, a taxpayer is permitted to exclude a certain portion of the annuity payments received from gross income. The amount of each payment excludable is determined by multiplying the payment received by what is referred to as the exclusion ratio. The exclusion ratio equals the taxpayer's investment in the annuity contract divided by the total expected benefits to be received under the contract. The amount received in excess of the excluded portion is includable in the annuitant's gross income.

EXAMPLE

Cal invests $10,000 in an annuity that is expected to pay a total of $25,000 in total benefits.

$$\frac{\$10,000}{\$25,000} = \frac{2}{5} = 40\% \text{ excludable. } 100\% - 40\% = 60\% \text{ includable.}$$

During the year Cal received $2,500 in payments from the annuity plan. Of the $2,500 received Cal can exclude $1,000 from gross income and must include $1,500 in gross income. The amount excludable is determined by multiplying the $2,500 received by the exclusion ratio of 40%.

3.10.1 Lifetime Annuities

Should an annuitant have a lifetime annuity and live longer than the life expectancy used in the contract, any amounts received after reaching the life expectancy will be entirely includable in the annuitant's gross income. Should the annuitant die before reaching his life expectancy no deduction for the unrecovered part of the investment in the contract is allowed.

3.10.2 Three-Year Rule

For employment related annuities which began payout on or before July 1, 1986, if the investment in the contract is recoverable within three years of the commencement of payments no inclusion in gross income is required until the entire amount of the investment in the contract is recovered. After such investment is recovered, all payments received under the contracts are includable in gross income.

3.11 Foreign Earned Income

A foreign national who becomes a U.S. resident is taxed on his worldwide income from the day he becomes a resident. If you are a U.S. citizen who works for any foreign employer, you must include your salary as income. The Internal Revenue Code does, however, allow taxpayers who are bona fide residents of a foreign country for a designated period to exclude at least a portion of their foreign earned income from gross income.

Review Questions

1. *What is an exclusion?*

    An exclusion is an item that is not included in gross income. An item received will be excluded from gross income due to not satisfying the definition of an inclusion in gross income, or being excluded under the U.S. Constitution or a provision of the Internal Revenue Code. (The Internal Revenue Code is the income tax law.)

2. *J receives a lump sum payment of life insurance, as a result of being the beneficiary of his father's life insurance policy. How much would J have to include in gross income as a result of receiving the lump-sum payment?*

J is permitted to exclude the entire amount received as a lump-sum payment as a result of the death of his father. Had J received an installment payment of the proceeds of the policy, he would have to include that part of each payment representing interest.

3. *Mr. and Mrs. Malone have $35,000 of adjusted gross income for 1991 and received $10,000 of social security benefits. How much, if any, of the social security benefits do the Malones have to include in their gross income if they file a joint return for 1991?*

The Malones would have to include $4,000 of the social security benefits received in their gross income as this is the lesser of 50% of the social security benefits they received and 50% of the excess. Their excess for the year is $8,000 [($35,000 + $5,000) − $32,000].

4. *Bill receives $1,000 of interest on a municipal bond and $500 of interest on a checking account. How much of the interest must Bill include in his gross income?*

Bill must include the $500 of interest he received on his checking account in his gross income.

5. *Bart invests $20,000 in an annuity that is to pay him $200 a month for 20 years. During the year he receives $1,800 of annuity payments. How much of these payments must Bart include in his gross income?*

Bart must include $1,050 of the annuity payments received in gross income. This total is included as it equals the amount received ($1,800) minus the excluded portion [$1,800 × ($20,000 ÷ $48,000)].

CHAPTER 4

INCLUSIONS IN GROSS INCOME

4.1 Definition of Inclusion

Items includable in gross income are referred to as inclusions in gross income.

4.2 Compensation

Most amounts received for services performed are includable in the taxpayer's gross income. Categories of payments generally falling into the inclusion category are salaries, wages, tips, bonuses, commissions, severance pay, and fees for services rendered.

4.2.1 Payment in Property

When a worker is given property rather than cash as compensation, the fair market value of the property is includable in the worker's gross income.

4.2.2 Bargain Purchases

In some instances, a worker may purchase an asset from his employer. In such cases, compensation is deemed to exist to the extent the fair market value of the asset purchased exceeds the amount paid for the asset.

EXAMPLE

Tim pays $25 for an asset valued at $100 from his employer. Tim has a $75 inclusion in gross income.

4.2.3 Special Rules

While generally the value of any benefit received by an employee is included in the employee's gross income certain exceptions exist. These exceptions include:

1) Certain fringe benefits as described in chapter 3.

2) **Meals and Lodging**—An employee may exclude from gross income the value of meals and lodging furnished on the business premises by the employer. For meals to be so excludable, such must be furnished for the convenience of the employer. For lodging to be excludable, the lodging must be required as a condition of employment.

3) **Clergy**—A clergyman can exclude a housing allowance provided by the congregation to the extent it is used for payments related to the housing, e.g., mortgage, utilities, and interest on the mortgage, but not to exceed the fair market value of the housing plus utilities.

4) **Restricted Compensation**—An employee who receives property that is subject to substantial risk of forfeiture or is nontransferable has an option. The employee can elect to include the fair market value of the property in gross income in the year of receipt or can wait to see if the restrictions lapse. As a general rule if no election is made and the restrictions lapse or terminate, fair market value of the property at the time of such lapse will be includable in the taxpayer's gross income in the year of lapse. If the taxpayer in fact forfeits the property due to not satisfying the conditions and does not make an election no inclusion in gross income is made.

4.3 Interest

Absent qualification for inclusion as interest on a state, municipal, or political subdivision bond or obligation interest must generally be included in gross income.

4.4 Rent

Rent is the payment to another for use of his or her property. Rent received is includable in the gross income of the lessor. When a tenant makes an improvement on the leased property such will not constitute rent unless serving as a rent substitute. Payments received by a lessor to cancel, modify, amend, or terminate a lease are treated as rent and included in the lessor's gross income.

4.5 Prizes and Awards

Generally, any prize or award received is included in gross income. An exclusion is allowed for a prize or award received for certain designated purposes, e.g., charitable, scientific, educational, civic, or literary, which the recipient received without entry into a contest and which the taxpayer assigned all the taxpayer's interest in to a government agency or charitable organization. An exclusion is also permitted to employees for safety and length of service awards to the extent of $400 of personal property (in some instances an award of up to a value of $1,600 is excludable).

4.6 Forgiveness of Debt

Cancellation of indebtedness by a creditor or satisfaction of a debt for less than the outstanding amount of the debt generally gives rise to an inclusion in gross the debtor's gross income.

4.6.1 Exceptions to the Above Treatment

When the debt is discharged in bankruptcy no inclusion in gross income is required if certain tax attributes are reduced by the taxpayer, e.g., basis or certain carryovers. Likewise, where the taxpayer is insolvent, discharge of a debt will not be included in the taxpayer's gross income if certain tax attributes are reduced unless the debtor is made solvent due to the discharge of the debt. Where made so solvent an inclusion in gross income is required to the extent of solvency.

Inclusion is also avoided if the discharge constitutes a gift by the creditor to the debtor. Absent a family relationship between the parties it is unlikely that such a gift will be found.

4.7 Illegal Income

Income, even if derived through an illegal act, is includable in gross income.

4.8 Gambling Income

Gambling income is includable to the extent it exceeds gambling expenses.

4.9 Unemployment Compensation

Any unemployment compensation received is includable in gross income.

4.10 Tax Benefit Rule

According to the tax benefit rule if a taxpayer derived a tax savings in a prior year due to a deduction or a credit, and recovers the amount or some part thereof giving rise to the deduction or credit in a subsequent year, the recovery will have tax significance in the subsequent year. If a deduction was taken, the recovery will be included in gross income. If a credit was taken the recovery will result in an increase in the taxpayer's tax liability.

4.11 Typical Corporate Distributions

The most common type of corporate distribution is the ordinary dividend. Such amounts are reported as ordinary income by the shareholder.

A corporate distribution of property or cash to its shareholder will generally be characterized as an ordinary dividend to the extent it is covered by earnings and profits of the corporation allocable to the distribution. To the extent the distribution exceeds such allocable share of earnings and profits it will be considered a return of capital. A return of capital goes first toward recovery of the shareholder's basis in the shareholder's stock, and to the extent exceeding such investment will give rise to capital gain includable in gross income.

EXAMPLE

Y is a shareholder with a stock basis of $10,000 in M Corporation and receives a distribution of $25,000 from M Corporation. M has earnings and profits of $9,000. As a result of the distribution Y has a $9,000 ordinary dividend, a $10,000 return of capital, and a $6,000 capital gain.

Review Questions

1. *What is an inclusion in gross income?*

   An inclusion in gross income is an item that must be included in gross income. Typically, such an item is characterized by its resulting in an increase in the taxpayer's net worth and being an item not already held by the taxpayer.

2. *Give five examples of an inclusion in gross income.*

   Wages, rent, illegal income, alimony received, and interest on a savings account.

3. *Bob receives $500 in stock from his employer subject to the condition that if Bob leaves the employ within five years of re-*

ceipt of the stock he must return the stock to his employer. How much must Bob include in gross income in the year of receipt of the stock as a result of such receipt?

Bob need not include anything in gross income in the year of receipt of the stock because it is restricted compensation. If Bob wants to, he can, however, elect to include $500 value in gross income in the year of receipt.

4. *Jim goes to the racetrack and wins $500. How much must Jim include in gross income as a result of his winnings?*

Jim must include the entire $500 in his gross income.

5. *Jack receives $2,000 in unemployment compensation. How much of the unemployment compensation must Jack include in his gross income?*

Jack must include the entire $2,000 in his gross income.

6. *A corporation distributes $10,000 to its sole shareholder for the year. For the year of distribution the corporation has $9,000 of earnings and profits. How much of the distribution must the shareholder report as ordinary dividend for the year of receipt?*

The shareholder must report as ordinary dividend the portion of the distribution received covered by earnings and profits. In this instance, such amount is $9,000. The remaining $1,000 received by the shareholder constitutes a return of capital.

CHAPTER 5

GAINS AND LOSSES

5.1 What is a Gain or Loss?

A sale or exchange of property generally produces a gain or loss. A gain is produced if the taxpayer's amount realized on the transaction exceeds the taxpayer's adjusted basis in the asset transferred. Whereas a loss is produced if the amount realized is less than the basis of the asset transferred.

To compute a gain or loss the following formula is used:

Amount Realized – Adjusted Basis = Gain (Loss)

As a general rule a gain resulting from a transaction is included in the taxpayer's gross income and a loss deductible toward adjusted gross income.

5.2 Realized Gain or Loss

A gain or loss determined pursuant to the above formula is considered realized.

5.3 Recognition of Gain or Loss

A gain or loss which is reported for tax purposes is considered a gain or loss recognized. Usually a gain or loss realized is also a gain or loss recognized, but this is not always the case. For example, a loss realized on the disposition of personal use property, e.g., one's stereo, is not recognized for tax purposes, and gains or losses realized on nontaxable exchanges are not typically recognized

5.4 The Fundamental Formula and Its Terms

In order to compute gain or loss on a transaction, it is necessary to understand the meaning of the terms "amount realized" and "adjusted basis" and how such are determined.

Amount Realized—The amount realized on a sale or exchange is the amount received on such sale or exchange. The amount received on a sale or exchange is usually the sum of the cash received plus the fair market value of other property received plus any liability relief obtained on the transaction.

Adjusted Basis—A taxpayer's adjusted basis in an asset is the amount the taxpayer is entitled to recover free of tax upon a disposition of the asset. A taxpayer's initial basis in an asset depends upon the manner in which the asset was acquired. Such original basis is then adjusted upward or downward for certain costs or events.

5.5 Adjustments to Basis

The basis of an asset is increased for: improvements, certain costs incurred in acquiring the asset, e.g., title insurance, recording costs, abstract costs, transportation costs, attorney fees, installation charges, purchase commissions, and survey expenditures.

Basis is decreased for the following items: depreciation, depletion, tax free recoveries of capital on the asset, and deductible casualty and theft losses.

In order to determine the adjusted basis of an asset not only is it important to determine the adjustments to basis but the original

31

basis to which these adjustments must be made. The remainder of this chapter will focus upon the effect on basis of how an asset was acquired.

5.6 Purchase of Property

If property is purchased, the purchase price is the beginning basis. Oftentimes taxpayers acquire multiple assets in the same transaction without allocating the purchase price to the individual assets acquired. In such instances it is necessary to make such allocation in order to determine gain or loss on disposition of one of the assets so acquired as well as such important tax items as depreciation on the assets.

To allocate a single purchase price to multiple assets the purchase price must be multiplied by a fraction, the numerator of which is the fair market value to which the allocation is to be made and the denominator of which is the total fair market value of the assets acquired in the transaction.

EXAMPLE

Bill acquires several assets in a single transaction for $10,000. The total fair market value of the assets is $12,000. Bill wants to allocate part of the purchase price to one of the assets acquired in order to determine its basis. The fair market value of this asset is $6,000. Bill's basis in the asset is $5,000 [$10,000 multiplied by ($6,000 divided by $12,000)].

5.7 Property Received as Compensation

When property is received as compensation, the fair market value of the property received will be the taxpayer's original basis in the asset.

5.8 Property Received Incident to Divorce or Separation

When property is received incident to a divorce or separation, the recipient will acquire a basis in the asset equal to the basis of the transferor at the time of the transfer.

5.9 Property Received as a Gift

In determining the basis to a donee of property received as a gift, if the donor's basis in the property at the time of the gift is less than the fair market value of the property at the time of the gift, the donee's basis will be equal to the donor's basis plus the product of the gift tax resulting from the gift and the fair market value of the property minus the adjusted basis of the property divided by the fair market value of the property.

EXAMPLE

Father gives son stock as a graduation gift. At the time of the gift father has a basis in the stock of $15,000 and the stock has a fair market value of $20,000. Father paid a gift tax on the gift of $3,000. Son's basis is $15,750 [$15,000 plus ($5,000 divided by $20,000 multiplied by $3,000)].

If the fair market value of the gift property at the time of the gift is less than the donor's basis in the gift property and the donee sells the gift property for less than such fair market value, the donee's basis for computing loss will be the fair market value of the property. Should, however, the fair market value be lower than the donor's basis and the donee sells the property for an amount in between the donor's basis and the fair market value neither gain nor loss will be recognized by the donee on the sale.

5.10 Inheritance

Generally, the basis of an inherited asset is the fair market value of the asset on the date of the decedent's death. Should the estate qualify for use of the alternate valuation date and an appropriate election be made, the basis of an inherited asset will be the fair market value of the asset six months after the date of the decedent's death should the asset not be distributed within such six month period. If the alternative election date is elected and the asset distributed within the six month period following the date of the decedent's death, the basis of the asset will be the value of the asset on the date of distribution.

An exception to the above rules exists for assets which are bequeathed by the decedent back to a person who gave such assets to the decedent within the year preceding the decedent's death. In such instances the donor-heir will obtain a basis in the property equal to that which the decedent had in the property immediately before the decedent died.

5.11 Joint Tenancy with Rights of Survivorship

The joint tenancy with rights of survivorship is one form of multiple ownership. It is distinguished from other types of multiple ownership in that when one of the owners dies, his interest passes automatically over to the surviving joint tenant(s). The interest thus passing is included in the decedent's estate according to the date of death or alternate valuation date value if appropriate, and added to the basis of the surviving joint tenant(s) in the property. The value includable in the estate of the first to die of the joint tenants is based upon the percentage of the consideration for the asset provided by the decedent.

Where a joint tenancy is held between husband and wife, regardless of how much of the consideration either spouse provided, each one is treated for tax purposes as having contributed 50% of the consideration from the asset, and so 50% of the relevant value of the asset is included in the estate of the first to die and passes over to the survivor, to be added to the survivor's basis in the asset.

5.12 Taxable Exchange

An exchange is characterized as part of the consideration received by each party to the transaction, being a nonmonetary asset. Absent qualification under special tax rules as a nontaxable exchange, an exchange will give rise to recognized gain or loss. A recognized gain will be produced on a taxable exchange should the value of the property and other consideration received on the exchange exceed the basis of the assets transferred.

5.13 First-In-First-Out

A first-in-first-out approach is used to determine the basis of stock sold when the seller has purchased the same class of stock in the same corporation at different times and not indicated which particular shares of such stock have been sold.

EXAMPLE

J bought 500 shares of Z Corporation common stock in 1985 for $1,000 and another 500 shares of Z Corporation common stock in 1990 for $1,500. In 1991 J sold 500 shares of Z Corporation common stock but did not identify which shares he sold. Pursuant to the first-in-first-out rule, J's basis in the stock sold is considered to be $1,000, as this is the basis of the first 500 shares acquired by J which could make up the 500 shares sold.

5.14 Intellectual Property and Self-Constructed Assets

Only the out-of-pocket costs incurred in developing a patent or a self-constructed asset, which have not otherwise been deducted, can be included in the basis of such property. The value of the time of the inventor or creator of the self-constructed asset cannot be included in the basis of the asset.

Review Questions

1. *What is the formula for computing a gain or loss on the disposition of property?*

   The formula is: Amount realized minus adjusted basis of the asset sold or exchanged.

2. *Jill inherits an asset from her father. The father's adjusted basis in the asset at the time of his death was $10,000 and the fair market value of the asset $12,000. The executor of the estate elects the alternative valuation date. The asset is distributed three months after the date of the father's death. On the date of distribution the asset has a fair market value of $13,000. What is Jill's basis in the asset?*

   Jill's basis in the asset is $13,000 as the alternative valuation date was properly elected and the property was distributed within the six-month period following the date of death.

3. *Tom receives a stock from his father as a graduation gift. The fair market value of the stock on the date of the gift is $7,000, and the father's adjusted basis in it is $8,000. Tom sells the stock for $5,000 after receiving it. What is Tom's loss on the sale of the stock?*

   Tom's loss on the sale of the stock is $2,000. This results because in computing a loss on the sale of property received as a gift the donee must use as his (her) basis the lesser of the fair market value of the asset on the date of the gift or the donor's adjusted basis.

4. *Doug receives a car worth $5,000 from his employer as compensation. What must Doug include in gross income as a result of the receipt?*

   Doug must include $5,000 (the fair market value of the asset received minus consideration paid for it) in his gross income. This amount is treated as salary or wages received.

5. *F transfers a home with an adjusted basis of $50,000 to his former wife as part of a property settlement incident to divorce. The house is worth $60,000 at the time of the transfer. What is the wife's basis in the house received?*

The wife will obtain the transferor's basis in the house, in this scenario, $50,000.

6. *F transfers his home in which he has a basis of $35,000 to S for a building valued at $45,000. What is F's gain or loss on the transaction?*

The transaction constitutes a taxable exchange since it is not a like-kind exchange. In this instance F has a gain on the exchange of $10,000 as this is the amount by which the amount he received exceeds the adjusted basis of the asset he transferred.

CHAPTER 6

NONRECOGNITION

6.1 The Nontaxable Exchange

The tax law allows certain types of exchanges to qualify for nonrecognition of gain or loss. These transactions are all based upon the fundamental notion that it is improper to tax a taxpayer on a transaction which merely results in a continuation of the taxpayer's investment in the asset transferred. Transactions falling within the nonrecognition category include:

1) The exchange of certain life insurance policies.

2) The conversion of bonds.

3) The transfer of property solely in return for stock in a corporation in which the transferor possesses at least 80% of all classes of stock immediately after the exchange.

The principal type of nontaxable exchange, however, is the like-kind exchange.

6.2 The Like-Kind Exchange

Internal Revenue Code Section 1031 provides that the exchange of property held for investment or for use in the taxpayer's trade or business, for property to be held for investment or for use in the taxpayer's trade or business, is eligible for nonrecognition of gain or loss. Certain types of property are not eligible for such nonrecognition treatment. Ineligible property includes property held primarily for personal use, property held primarily for sale, e.g., inventory, partnership interests, stock, U.S. currency for foreign currency, and livestock of different sexes.

Where a like-kind exchange is undergone, a loss realized on the exchange will not be recognized. Instead the basis of the asset transferred will generally become the basis of the asset received and a loss will later be recognized if and when the asset received is disposed of.

Gain realized on a like-kind exchange will be recognized to the extent the taxpayer receives boot on the exchange. Boot is defined as non-like-kind property received on the exchange.

EXAMPLE

Mat exchanges a tractor he uses in his farming business and which has a basis of $5,000 to John in return for a tractor valued at $6,000 and $2,000 in cash. The exchange qualifies as a like-kind exchange. Mat must recognize at least some portion of the gain realized due to having received some boot on the transaction. In this scenario, Mat has a realized gain of $3,000 [($6,000 plus $2,000) minus $5,000], and a recognized gain of $2,000 since this is the lesser of the gain realized and the boot received.

In some instances a taxpayer will obtain relief of a liability, e.g., a mortgage, in a like-kind exchange. In determining the amount of boot a taxpayer has received in a like-kind exchange, liability relief is generally treated as boot received. Where the taxpayer is relieved of a liability and takes responsibility for a liability of the other party to the transaction, only the amount by which the liability relief obtained exceeds the liability taken on, will be treated as boot resulting from the taxpayer's liability relief.

Basis—In determining the basis of like-kind property received in a like-kind exchange the following steps are undergone:

	Basis of the like-kind property transferred
Minus	Boot Received
Plus	Gain Recognized
Plus	Additional consideration transferred

6.3 Involuntary Conversions

An involuntary conversion occurs when a taxpayer loses or surrenders an asset through no voluntary action on the taxpayer's part. There exists three basic types of involuntary conversions. These are condemnations, casualties, and thefts.

6.3.1 Gain

If certain criteria are satisfied, a taxpayer is permitted to defer the recognition of gain realized on an involuntary conversion. These criteria are:

1) **Acquisition of Qualified Replacement Property**—As a general rule qualified replacement property is property that is similar or related in function or use to the asset involuntarily converted, e.g., a copy machine replaced by a copy machine. When the involuntary conversion property is a condemnation of real estate used in the taxpayer's trade or business, or real estate held for investment, qualified replacement is defined as either real estate to be used in the taxpayer's trade or business, or real estate held for investment.

2) **Acquisition of the Qualified Replacement Property Must Be Timely**—The maximum time within which replacement may generally be made is usually two years from the last day of the taxable year wherein the taxpayer realized gain on the involuntary conversion. Where the involuntary conversion is a condemnation of real estate used in the taxpayer's trade or business or held for investment, the replacement is usually limited to three years from the last

day of the taxable year in which the taxpayer realized gain on the involuntary conversion.

3) **Election**—The taxpayer must make an appropriate election on the tax return for the year in which gain is realized indicating the intent to use the deferral of recognition of gain in order to avoid having to recognize all of the gain realized on the involuntary conversion.

4) **The Cost of Replacement Property Must Exceed the Basis of the Involuntary Converted Property**.

Determination of Gain Recognized—If the above criteria are satisfied, should the qualified replacement property cost more than the amount realized on the involuntary conversion, none of the gain realized on the involuntary conversion need be recognized. Should, however, the cost of the qualified replacement property be greater than the basis of the involuntarily converted property but less than the amount realized, the excess of the amount realized over the cost of the replacement property constitutes recognized gain.

6.3.2 Basis

The basis of the qualified replacement property equals its cost minus the gain realized but not recognized on the involuntary conversion.

EXAMPLE

Jean's hotel in which she had a basis of $1,000,000 was condemned by the city. Jean received a condemnation of $1,250,000. She immediately bought another hotel for $1,100,000 and made an appropriate election on her tax return for nonrecognition of gain. As a result Jean has a recognized gain of $150,000 ($1,250,000 amount realized minus $1,100,000 cost of qualified replacement property). Her basis in the qualified replacement property is $1,000,000 ($1,100,000 minus $100,000 gain realized but not recognized). Note that if Jean had acquired qualified replacement property costing $1,250,000 or more, none of the gain realized would be recognized and the basis of the qualified replacement property would be determined by subtracting $250,000 from the cost of the replacement property.

6.4 Age 55 or Older Exclusion

The tax law permits an exclusion of up to a maximum of $125,000 of gain realized from gross income on the sale of the taxpayer's principal residence if the following criteria are satisfied:

1) The taxpayer is at least 55 years of age as of the date of the sale.

2) The residence sold has been the taxpayer's principal residence for at least three of the five calendar years preceding the sale. For taxpayers who are placed in a qualified institution, the taxpayer need only live in the residence for one year preceding the sale for the residence to be considered the taxpayer's principal residence.

3) The taxpayer must not have previously elected non-recognition of gain under this provision. Note that some relief from this nonprior election rule exists for elections made before 1978. In keeping with the logic of this rule the taxpayer must make an election with the tax return for the year for which the exclusion is desired in order to utilize it.

Where the taxpayer is married and attempting to use the exclusion on a joint return, it is necessary that one of the spouses meet each of the three stated criteria. Should a taxpayer seek the exclusion and be married filing separately, the maximum exclusion is limited to $62,500.

6.5 Rollover of Principal Residence

Taxpayers are permitted to defer the recognition of gain realized on the sale of a principal residence when the taxpayer acquires and occupies another principal residence within two years before or after the sale producing the gain if the cost of the replacement residence is greater than the basis of the residence disposed of. A longer period is allowed for taxpayers in active military service or living abroad.

In computing the gain recognized on the sale of the replaced residence and the basis of the replacement residence the following steps are utilized:

	Selling Price of the Residence Sold
–	Selling Expenses
	Amount Realized
–	Adjusted Basis of the Residence Sold
	Realized Gain
	Amount Realized
–	Fixing Up Expenses
	Adjusted Selling Price
	Adjusted Selling Price
–	Cost of Replacement Residence
	Gain Recognized
	Gain Realized
–	Gain Recognized
	Gain Realized but Not Recognized
	Cost of New Residence
–	Gain Realized but Not Recognized
	Basis of Replacement Residence

As depicted in the previous formula, to the extent gain realized on the sale is not recognized, the basis of the replacement residence must be reduced. In applying the formula it is critical to understand the meaning of the term "fixing up" expenses. "Fixing up" expenses are expenses which are incurred in making the residence ready for sale that are not deducted nor otherwise capitalized and are for work done within the 90-day period before the sale contract is entered into and is paid for by the end of the 30-day period following the sale (closing).

Unlike the age-55-or-older exclusion, which must be elected in order to be qualified for, the rollover deferral rule applies automatically if qualified for.

Review Questions

1. *Taxpayer exchanges a computer used in his trade or business with an adjusted basis of $8,000 for a computer to be used in his business with a fair market value of $12,000. What is the taxpayer's realized and recognized gain on the transaction, and what is his basis in the computer received?*

   Taxpayer has a gain realized on the exchange of $4,000. None of the gain realized is recognized due to the exchange being a non-taxable exchange on which the taxpayer did not receive boot. It is a like-kind exchange, i.e., business computer for business computer. Since the taxpayer neither received nor transferred boot or other property on the exchange, the taxpayer will obtain a basis in the asset received equal to the basis of the asset transferred, i.e., $8,000.

2. *Bob exchanged land held for investment with a basis of $100,000 and subject to a mortgage of $50,000 for land to be held for investment with a fair market value of $110,000 subject to a mortgage of $30,000. What is Bob's gain recognized on the transaction?*

   Bob's gain recognized on the transaction is $20,000 as this is the lesser of the gain realized on the transaction [($110,000 plus

$50,000) minus ($100,000 plus $30,000)] and the boot received ($50,000 minus $30,000).

3. *The state condemned taxpayer's farm, awarding taxpayer $100,000. The taxpayer's basis in the farm was $75,000. Immediately after receiving the condemnation award the taxpayer acquired a new farm for $90,000, and made an appropriate election on his tax return for nonrecognition of gain. What is the taxpayer's gain recognized on the transaction and what is the taxpayer's basis in the new farm?*

    Taxpayer's gain recognized on the condemnation is $10,000 ($100,000 condemnation award minus $90,000 cost of replacement property). The basis of the replacement farm is $75,000 ($90,000 cost minus $15,000 gain realized but not recognized).

4. *How old must a taxpayer be to qualify for the $125,000 ($62,500 for married filing separately) exclusion of gain on the sale of principal residence?*

    The taxpayer must be 55 years of age at the time of the sale to be eligible for the exclusion of gain on sale of principal residence.

5. *Taxpayer, age 32, sold his principal residence for a $20,000 gain realized. The cash amount realized on the sale was $75,000, and the taxpayer incurred no fixing up expenses. Three months after the sale the taxpayer purchased a new principal residence for $70,000, how much of the gain realized must be recognized by the taxpayer? And what is the taxpayer's basis in the new principal residence?*

    The taxpayer must recognize $5,000 of the gain realized, as this is the amount by which the adjusted sales price (note due to the lack of fixing up expenses the adjusted sales price equals the amount realized) exceeds the cost of the replacement residence. ($75,000 sales price less $70,000 cost of new residence equals $5,000.) The taxpayer's basis in the new principal residence is $55,000. ($70,000 cost of new residence less $15,000 unrecognized gain equals $55,000.)

CHAPTER 7

CAPITAL GAINS AND LOSSES

7.1 Treatment of Capital Gains and Losses

As a general rule, if a taxpayer has a gain recognized on a transaction, capital gain treatment is desired. This results because capital gain is subject to a lower maximum tax rate than ordinary income under the current law and can be used to offset capital losses without limitation. In contrast, where a loss recognized exists, taxpayers prefer that the loss be accorded ordinary loss treatment. This preference lies in the fact that while capital losses can offset capital gains without limitation, capital losses that remain after capital losses are netted against capital gain can only be used to offset a limited amount of ordinary income—this amount being $3,000 ($1,500 in the case of taxpayers filing married filing separately).

7.2 Capital Assets: What are They?

The Internal Revenue Code defines capital assets by stating that such include all assets other than inventory; property held for sale to customers in the ordinary course of the taxpayer's trade or business; depreciable property used in the taxpayer's trade or business; art, musical compositions, and literary works in the hands of the person who created the work and persons who obtained a basis in such work from the creator, e.g., a donee; accounts and notes receivable obtained in the ordinary course of the taxpayer's trade or business;

and U.S. government publications. It is helpful to note that capital assets generally fall into two categories, these being personal use property, e.g., one's stereo used for personal purposes, and investment property that is not depreciable.

7.3 Holding Period

Each year in determining their tax, taxpayers must see what recognized gains and losses from the disposition of capital assets they have for the year. These gains and losses must be separated into groups of short-term capital gains, short-term capital losses, long-term capital gains, and long-term capital losses. The determination of which group a gain or loss falls in depends on the taxpayer's holding period in the asset. An asset is considered to be held long term if the taxpayer's holding period in the asset exceeds one year. Should the holding period be one year or less, the asset is considered to have been held short term.

7.4 Determination of Holding Period

The determination of a taxpayer's holding period in an asset depends upon how the taxpayer acquired the asset. If the asset was acquired by purchase, the holding period begins on the date after acquisition. The effect on holding period of other common methods of acquisition are:

1) **Inheritance**—A capital asset that is acquired by the taxpayer through inheritance is automatically considered to be held long term.

2) **Gift**—The determination of holding period for a donee in property received as a gift depends upon the basis the donee uses to compute gain or loss on the disposition of the asset. If the donor's basis (plus an adjustment for gift tax paid if applicable) is used, the donee's holding period will include the holding period of the donor. Should the basis used be the fair market value of the property on the date of the gift, the donee's holding period will begin on the date of the gift.

3) **Rollover of Principal Residence and Nontaxable Exchange**—In the case of a rollover of principal residence, the taxpayer's holding period in the replacement residence will include the holding period of the residence disposed of. The holding period of an asset obtained in a nontaxable exchange will include the holding period of the asset transferred.

4) **First-In-First-Out Property**—The basis of which is determined under the first-in-first-out rule, will have its holding period determined by using the holding period associated with the basis used.

5) **Option**—The holding period of property acquired pursuant to exercise of an option begins on the date of exercise of the option, and does not include the period the option is held.

7.5 Netting

Each year a schedule D of the taxpayer's return, capital gains and losses for the year are netted. Long-term capital gains are netted against long-term capital losses, and short-term capital gains are netted against short-term capital losses. If each of these nettings produces a gain, the total gain is generally included in gross income. If each netting produces a loss, the total loss is deductible toward adjusted gross income subject to the limitations mentioned in 7.1. Where both are a loss, the short-term capital loss is to be used to the extent allowable before the long-term capital loss can be used. If one of the nettings produces a gain and one a loss, the gain and loss are then netted together with the difference taking on the character of the greater absolute figure.

7.6 Section 1231 Property: What is It?

The tax law provides certain assets with the potential of getting long-term capital gain treatment if there is a gain and ordinary loss in the case of a loss. These assets and their treatment are prescribed in

Section 1231. Assets falling within Section 1231 include:

1) Real estate and depreciable property used in the taxpayer's trade or business or held for the production of rental or royalty income and held for more than one year.

2) Capital assets held for more than one year which have been involuntarily converted.

3) Certain livestock and unharvested crops which have been sold or exchanged.

4) Timber and coal or iron ore which meet certain conditions.

7.7 The Section 1231 Netting Process

In determining the tax consequence of 1231 assets which have been disposed during the taxable year, the following three steps are utilized:

1) **Recapture**—Where a depreciable Section 1231 asset is disposed of in a transaction producing a gain recognized, a certain amount of the gain may have to be "recaptured" and treated as ordinary income. The gain recaptured is to be excluded from further Section 1231 netting.

2) Net gains and losses from thefts and casualties of Section 1231 trade or business property. If the netting produces a net gain, the net gain is to be placed in the third step of the netting process; however, should the netting produce a loss, the loss will be treated as an ordinary loss and typically be deductible in full toward adjusted gross income.

3) Net all the gains and losses from Section 1231 assets not reflected in steps 1 or 2, with the net gain, if any, produced in step 2 and the gain on the disposition of Section 1231 property not recaptured in step 1. If the netting produces a net gain, the net gain is treated as a long-term capital gain. If the netting produces a net loss, the loss will be treated as an ordinary loss deductible in full toward adjusted gross income.

7.8 Insight into Recapture

In ascertaining the amount recaptured by an individual on the disposition of a Section 1231 asset, the following rules apply:

1) **Section 1239 Recapture**—Pursuant to this rule all gain on the sale or exchange of a depreciable 1231 asset between related parties must be recaptured as ordinary income.

2) **Section 1245 Recapture**—This recapture rule applies to dispositions of depreciable Section 1231 personal property, e.g., equipment and machinery, and depreciable Section 1231 nonresidential real estate which has been depreciated under an accelerated method. Pursuant to this rule depreciation must be recaptured to the extent of the lesser of the gain recognized or the depreciation taken on the asset. Depreciable personal property is property that is tangible and moveable as well as depreciable.

EXAMPLE

Mike has a computer which he uses in his business. Mike acquired the computer in 1988 for $10,000 and has taken depreciation of $4,000 on it. This year he sold the computer for $12,000. As a result of the sale, Mike has $6,000 of gain recognized. Four-thousand dollars of this gain is recaptured as ordinary income, as this is the lesser of the gain recognized and depreciation taken, and the remaining $2,000 of gain is treated as Section 1231 gain to be placed in the third step of the Section 1231 netting process.

3) **Section 1250 Recapture**—This recapture rule applies to Section 1231 depreciable residential real estate, e.g., an apartment building, and depreciable nonresidential real estate which is depreciated under a straight-line method. Pursuant to this rule, depreciation is to be recaptured to the extent of the lesser of the gain recognized and the depreciation taken in excess of straight-line on the asset. As a result of this rule, should a taxpayer use the straight-line method to depreciate real estate constituting Section 1231 prop-

erty, none of the gain recognized on the disposition will be recaptured.

7.9 Special Characterization Rules

While stock is generally treated as a capital asset, the tax law prescribes some exceptions to this treatment. For example, when the stock is considered to be that of a collapsible corporation, gain on the sale of the stock will be treated as ordinary income. Likewise, when the sale is considered tantamount to inventory in the hands of the taxpayer, gain on its sale will be treated as ordinary income. Should the stock be considered that held in a qualified small business corporation, loss on its sale is eligible for ordinary loss treatment, if certain criteria are met. To qualify for this preferential treatment as a small business corporation, the corporation must generally have had no more than $1,000,000 of paid-in capital since its inception and the shareholder must be the original holder of the stock upon its issuance. When such criteria are met, a loss recognized on the disposition of the stock of up to $100,000 during a year by a married taxpayer filing jointly can be treated as an ordinary loss and up to $50,000 of loss to be recognized for a year can be treated as ordinary loss by taxpayers of other filing statuses.

The tax law also provides a break for subdividers of real estate by prescribing that if certain conditions are met, gain on the sale of not more than five lots by the end of the tax year will be treated as capital gain.

Review Questions

1. *Which of the following are capital assets: refrigerator used in the taxpayer's home, computer used in business, or inventory?*

   The only one of these assets constituting a capital asset is the refrigerator used in the taxpayer's home.

2. *Why is an ordinary loss considered preferable to a capital loss?*

   Because an ordinary loss can generally be deducted in full

toward adjusted gross income; whereas a capital loss after offsetting capital gain can only be used to offset a limited amount of ordinary income. (At this writing, $3,000.)

3. *Jack inherited stock from his father on January 1, 1991, and sold it on January 10, 1991. Will Jack's gain or loss on the sale be a long-term or short-term capital loss?*

A gain or loss on the sale of an inherited asset is automatically treated as a long-term capital gain or loss regardless of how long the taxpayer actually held the asset.

4. *Bill bought an apartment building for $500,000 on which he took $200,000 of depreciation using an accelerated method of depreciation. Depreciation using the straight line method over the same period would have been $150,000. Bill sold the building for $600,000. What is Bill's gain or loss on the sale and how is such gain or loss characterized?*

Bill has a gain on the sale of $300,000 ($600,000 amount realized minus $300,000 adjusted basis). Of the $300,000 of gain, $50,000 is treated as depreciation recaptured and ordinary income due to such being the lesser of the gain recognized and the depreciation taken in excess of straight line. The remaining $250,000 gain is characterized as Section 1231 gain.

5. *What is the benefit of having stock be considered qualified small business corporation stock rather than regular stock?*

Usually a loss recognized on the sale of regular stock is treated as a capital loss and subject to limitation as to its use in offsetting ordinary income. In contrast, a substantial portion (if not all) of the loss on the sale of qualified small business corporation stock is allowed to be treated as an ordinary loss and thus avoids the limitations befalling capital losses.

CHAPTER 8

DEDUCTIONS TOWARD ADJUSTED GROSS INCOME

8.1 Deductions toward and from Adjusted Gross Income

There exist two basic categories of deductions—those toward and those from adjusted gross income. Of these categories, deductions toward adjusted gross income are the more valuable because taxpayers benefit from such deductions even if they do not itemize. In contrast, taxpayers only derive a benefit from itemized deductions if their itemized deductions exceed their standard deduction amount. In addition, even should they itemize, taxpayers do not reap the full benefit of a deduction from an itemized deduction because they would be entitled to deduct at least their standard deduction amount anyway.

8.2 Alimony

Alimony paid is a major type of deduction toward adjusted gross income. In general, to constitute alimony for tax purposes, the following criteria must be met: The payment must be considered made in cash, the payment must not be considered child support or some other type of payment not includable in the gross income of the recipient, and the spouses cannot cohabit after the commencement of payments.

8.2.1 Recapture

Should the amount of alimony paid annually decline by a certain prescribed amount within the first three years of payment, a certain amount of alimony paid must be recaptured. The amount recaptured is deducted toward the adjusted gross income of the recipient spouse and included in the gross income of the payor spouse in the return for the third year following commencement of the payment of alimony.

8.3 Penalties on Premature Withdrawal of Time Bearing Deposits

Any penalty incurred on the withdrawal of a savings type account prior to maturity, e.g., a certificate of deposit or tax sheltered annuity, will be deductible toward the taxpayer's adjusted gross income.

8.4 Losses on Dispositions of Property

A loss recognized on the sale or exchange of property is deductible toward adjusted gross income. Likewise, a theft or casualty loss incurred with regard to trade or business property is deductible toward adjusted gross income. Note that in some instances the amount that can be deducted in a taxable year may be limited due to the character of the loss, e.g., in the case of a capital loss.

8.5 Individual Retirement Account Contributions

Qualified Individual Retirement Account contributions are deductible toward adjusted gross income. The maximum amount that can be deducted by a working taxpayer is limited to the lesser of $2,000 or the taxpayer's earned income for the year. In the case of a spouse who makes less than $250 of earned income for the year, the tax law permits a maximum deduction of $250.

The maximum deduction allowed for an IRA contribution is phased out if the taxpayer is considered an active participant in an employer's retirement plan and has adjusted gross income in excess of a certain amount.

8.6 Health Insurance Premiums

For tax years beginning before January 1, 1992, the tax law permits 25% of the health insurance premiums, paid by self-employed taxpayers on behalf of themselves or their family members, to be allowed as a deduction toward adjusted gross income.

8.7 Self-Employment Taxes

Fifty percent of self-employment taxes paid by a self-employed taxpayer are deductible toward AGI.

8.8 Deductible Expenses of the Sole Proprietor or Self-Employed Person

As a general rule, trade or business expenses of a self-employed person or sole proprietor that are ordinary and necessary, connected with the trade or business, paid or incurred during the taxable year, and which are neither required to be capitalized or connected with the production of tax exempt income are deductible toward adjusted gross income. The following is a list of some such frequently encountered expenses:

1) Compensation paid to workers

2) Rent for the rental of property used in the trade or business

3) Advertising costs

4) Supplies

5) Premiums paid for insurance of a business asset

6) Fees paid to attorneys or accountants for certain work concerning the business

7) Certain travel and transportation expenses

8) Certain meals and entertainment expenses (limited to 80% of the qualified expense paid or incurred)

9) Certain educational expenses

10) Utilities expense

11) Interest expense related to the acquisition of assets for use in the trade or business

12) Depreciation expense

13) Section 179 expense

14) Qualified Research and Experimental Expense to the extent a credit is not taken for such expense

15) The cost of business gifts limited to $25 a person and advertising gifts limited to $4 a person

16) The cost of certain employee safety and achievement awards up to a limited extent

17) Property taxes with regard to trade or business property

8.9 Clarification of Certain Expenses

Travel—The term "travel" encompasses a variety of different expenses paid or incurred in the course of travel. Such costs include the cost of lodging, dry cleaning, taxis or the rental of a car, meals and entertainment, and going to and from the location. In general, if the travel is within the U.S. and it is primarily for business purposes, the entire cost of the trip is deductible. If the trip is outside the U.S., and if the trip is at least 75% for business, the entire cost of the trip is deductible; otherwise, the deductible amount of the trip is determined based upon the percentage of the time spent at the location for business purposes. With regard to other expenses, e.g., dry cleaning, taxi fares, and long distance phone bills, the expense if it can be established as related to the taxpayer's trade or business, such expense will also be deductible—but only 80% of such expenses are deductible. Lodging is deductible in an amount corresponding to the percentage of time the taxpayer is at the location for trade or business purposes.

Transportation Expenses—The cost of commuting is not generally deductible. The cost of going from one's place of business to a customer or client or from a place of business to another place of business is deductible.

Educational Expenses—To qualify for deduction the education must be related to the taxpayer's trade or business and improve or maintain the taxpayer's skill in his work while neither qualifying the taxpayer for a new trade or business or, in the case of an employee, enabling the employee to meet the minimum requirements of his present job.

Home Office Expenses—Certain home office expenses can qualify for deduction toward adjusted gross income; but in order to qualify, a certain portion of the home must be used regularly and exclusively as the principal place of such trade or business.

8.10 Expenses Related to the Production of Rental or Royalty Income

Expenses paid or incurred for the production of rental or royalty income constitute a major category of deductions toward adjusted gross income. Many of these expenses are similar to those encountered when dealing with a trade or business. These include:

1) Depreciation

2) Interest expense

3) Advertising expense

4) Management expense

5) Certain insurance expense

6) Property taxes

7) Repairs and maintenance expense

8) Travel to check on the upkeep of the premises if in a different geographic location

9) Utilities paid for by the landlord

8.11 Reimbursed Employee Business Expenses

Generally, to the extent reimbursed under a reimbursement or expense allowance arrangement, employee business expenses are deductible toward adjusted gross income.

Review Questions

1. *Which is preferable, a deduction toward adjusted gross income or an itemized deduction?*

    A deduction toward adjusted gross income is preferable as such can generally be used in full and provide a tax savings benefit.

    In contrast, an itemized deduction will only provide a tax savings benefit if the taxpayer's total allowable itemized deductions exceed the taxpayer's standard deduction amount and, even then, do not produce a complete tax savings benefit as the taxpayer would have been entitled to use the standard deduction amount anyway.

2. *List three types of deductions toward adjusted gross income not related to the taxpayer's trade or business or the holding of property for the production of rental or royalty income?*

    Alimony paid, a loss on a taxable exchange or sale of property, and 25% of health insurance premiums paid by a self-employed person for coverage on himself or a dependent.

3. *Brent, a librarian, attends law school in hopes of becoming a lawyer. Can he deduct the cost of his law school education?*

    Brent will not be allowed to deduct the cost of his law school as the education qualifies him for a new profession or job.

4. *Jim, a self-employed accountant, travels from Chicago to San Diego to see a client. He spends five days in San Diego of which four are spent on business and one on sightseeing. With regard to the trip, Jim spends $300 on plane fare, $400 on his hotel bill, and $150 on meals eaten alone. How much of these costs can be deducted by Jim?*

Of these costs Jim can deduct $716 ($300 for plane fare plus 80% of his hotel bill plus 80% of 80% of his meals eaten alone).

5. *What type of interest expense can a taxpayer deduct toward adjusted gross income?*

Interest expense on property held for the production of rental or royalty income as well as interest expense on property held for use in the taxpayer's trade or business if self-employed or a sole proprietor are deductible toward adjusted gross income.

CHAPTER 9

ITEMIZED DEDUCTIONS

9.1 Itemized Deductions

In order to benefit from itemized deductions, a taxpayer's total allowable itemized deductions must exceed the taxpayer's standard deduction amount. In order to determine a taxpayer's total allowable itemized deductions, expenses that fall into the category of itemized deductions as well as the application of special limits that may apply to such deductions must be ascertained.

9.2 Medical Expenses

The tax law defines medical expenses as any costs incurred for the diagnosis, cure, treatment, mitigation, or prevention of a disease to any bodily function or structure. Medical expenses are only includable in total allowable itemized deductions to the extent the total of such expenses exceed 7.5% of the taxpayer's adjusted gross income. Expenses commonly considered medical expenses include those for medical examinations, dentist and doctor bills, X-rays and other medical tests, prescription drugs, stays in the hospital, medical insurance, hearing aids, prescription glasses, and a wheelchair.

9.3 Charitable Contributions

As a general rule, taxpayers can include in their itemized deductions cash contributed and the basis of property donated to a qualified charitable organization. When the property donated is either stock or property that the organization can use in furtherance of its tax-exempt purpose and such property has been held long term, the full fair market value of the property can be considered the amount of the contribution.

9.3.1 Limitations

Typically, the maximum charitable contribution deduction a taxpayer can take for a taxable year is limited to 50% of the taxpayer's adjusted gross income. With regard to capital gain property, if the taxpayer takes the fair market value as the amount of the contribution deduction, the maximum deduction is limited to 30% of the taxpayer's adjusted gross income. This 30% limitation can be avoided if the taxpayer elects to treat his or her basis in the asset as the amount of the contribution (rather than its fair market value). If such election is made, the regular 50% will apply.

The 50% charitable contribution limit includes churches, public charities, and private operating foundations. A 30% limit applies to gifts other than "capital gain property" donated to veterans' organizations, fraternal organizations, nonprofit cemeteries, and certain private nonoperating foundations. A 20% limit applies to gifts of capital gain property to all qualified organizations other than a 50% limit on organizations.

9.4 Interest

Qualified Residential Interest—Usually interest on a taxpayer's home mortgage is deductible in full as an itemized deduction. No deduction is permitted, however, if the expense is considered a cost for services, e.g., a loan origination fee.

9.4.1 Consumer Interest

For tax years after 1990, no deduction is permitted for consumer interest. Interest typically falling within this category includes: most interest expense incurred on credit cards, that incurred with regard to consumer-type purchases, interest on student loans, and interest expense on underpayment of taxes.

9.4.2 Investment Interest Expense

For tax years after 1990, the maximum amount of investment interest expense deductible by a taxpayer is limited to the taxpayer's net investment income.

9.5 Taxes

State and local property taxes incurred on personal use property constitute an itemized deduction. Likewise, state and local income taxes are itemized deductions. With regard to property that is sold during the year, the deduction for property taxes must be allocated between the buyer and seller based on the percentage of the year in which each had an interest in the asset.

9.6 Moving Expenses

Moving-related expenses are eligible for treatment as an itemized deduction if two tests are satisfied:

1) **Time Test**—If the taxpayer is an employee, the taxpayer must live and work in the geographic area to which the move was made for at least 39 weeks out of the 52-week period following the move. If the taxpayer is self-employed, the taxpayer must live and work in the area to which the move was made for at least 78 weeks out of the 104-week period following the move.

2) **Distance Test**—The area to which the taxpayer has moved must be at least 35 miles nearer to the taxpayer's new

place of business than the taxpayer's old residence would be to the new place of business.

9.6.1 Allowable Moving Expenses

If the above tests are satisfied, the taxpayer may include in deductible moving expense the following types of moving related expenses:

1) The costs of moving household items and personal belongings.

2) The costs of traveling to the new residence (including meals and lodging).

3) The costs of househunting after acquiring the new job.

4) The costs of meals and lodging while residing in temporary lodgings in the geographic area to which moved while waiting to move (up to a maximum of 30 days) to permanent lodging.

5) The costs of selling the taxpayer's old residence and purchasing the new residence.

With regard to the above items, only 80% of the meals allowed are includable in the moving expense deduction. In addition, the maximum includable for items 3 and 4 combined is limited to $3,000 ($1,500 in the case of a taxpayer married filing separately). Items 3, 4, and 5 combined are limited to a maximum of $3,000 ($1,500 in the case of a taxpayer married filing separately).

9.7 Tier Two Itemized Deductions

The tax law requires that certain deductions falling within the itemized deduction classification be aggregated and only be permitted to be deductible to the extent their total exceeds 2% of the taxpayer's adjusted gross income. This group of itemized deductions has come to be known as "Tier Two Itemized Deductions." Deductions falling into this category include:

1) Unreimbursed employee business expenses

2) Employee business expenses reimbursed under a nonaccountable plan

3) Unreimbursed outside salesperson's expenses

4) Outside salesperson's business expenses reimbursed under a nonaccountable plan

5) Safety deposit box rental fees

6) Tax preparation, advisory, and determination fees

7) Fees for investment advice, collection, and management services (not pertaining to property producing tax exempt income)

8) Investment oriented publications

9) Subscriptions to investment periodicals

10) Union and professional dues

11) The cost of buying and maintaining uniforms or work attire not suitable for regular wear

12) Subscriptions related to area of employment

13) Employee educational expenses

With regard to the above expenses, the same definitions that apply to an expense for a self-employed person or sole proprietor apply also to an employee. Likewise, the 80% limitation that applies to qualified meal and entertainment expenses that applies to a sole proprietor or self-employed person applies to employees.

EXAMPLE

Bill has $75,000 of adjusted gross income for the taxable year and $3,000 of tier 2 itemized deductions. Bill may include $1,500 of the tier 2 itemized deductions to his total allowable itemized deductions [$3,000 − .02 ($75,000)].

Review Questions

1. *What must exist in order for a taxpayer to enjoy a benefit from itemizing his (her) deductions?*

    The taxpayer's total allowable itemized deductions must exceed the taxpayer's standard deduction amount.

2. *What is the significance of a taxpayer's adjusted gross income in determining the taxpayer's total allowable itemized deductions?*

    Many expenses can only be included in the taxpayer's total allowable itemized deductions to the extent exceeding a certain percentage of the taxpayer's adjusted gross income, e.g., medical expenses, tier two miscellaneous itemized deductions, and casualty and theft losses concerning personal use property. Other amounts, meanwhile, can only be included in total allowable itemized deductions up to a maximum equal to a certain percentage of the taxpayer's adjusted gross income, e.g., charitable contributions.

3. *Jack has $30,000 of adjusted gross income for the year. During the year he incurred $2,500 of medical expenses. How much of the medical expenses can Jack include in his total allowable itemized deductions?*

    Jack can include $250 of the medical expenses in his itemized deductions as this is the amount by which the medical expenses he incurred exceed 7.5% of his adjusted gross income.

4. *A taxpayer bought a pair of tickets from the church to the annual church picnic for $150 each. The fair market value of the tickets was $10 each. What is the taxpayer's charitable contribution?*

    The taxpayer's charitable contribution is $280 as this is the amount paid by the taxpayer for the tickets in excess of the actual fair market value of the tickets.

5. *A taxpayer with adjusted gross income of $50,000 gave a $27,000 cash contribution to his college alma mater. How should the taxpayer treat the contribution for tax purposes?*

The taxpayer may include $25,000 of the contribution in his itemized deductions for the year of the contribution as this is 50% of his adjusted gross income. The remaining $2,000 of the amount contributed may be carried forward for a period of up to five years.

6. *A house was sold by Rudy to Bob on February 1, 1991. The property tax for the year was $3,000 which was entirely paid by Bob. What is the property tax deduction allocable to Rudy? To Bob?*

The property tax deduction is allocated to the parties based upon the percentage of the tax year each party to the sale owned the asset. Rudy, therefore, is entitled to a property tax deduction of $255 [$3,000 multiplied by (31 divided by 365)]. Bob, meanwhile, is entitled to a property tax deduction of $2,745 [$3,000 multiplied by (334 divided by 365)].

7. *The Marcuses, a married couple, moved from Mobile, Alabama, to New York City due to Mr. Marcus getting a job transfer. The Marcuses incurred $2,500 of househunting expenses and costs for temporary quarters (categories 3 and 4 costs) in making the move. How much of these costs can the Marcuses include in their itemized deductions?*

The Marcuses can include a total of $1,500 of these expenses in their itemized deductions.

8. *The Smiths have adjusted gross income of $35,000 for the year. During the year, they incurred $500 in tax preparation fees, a safety deposit rental fee of $50, and union dues of $250. How much of these costs can the Smiths include in their itemized deductions?*

These expenses fall within the category of itemized deductions that must be aggregated and are only includable in itemized deductions to the extent exceeding 2% of the taxpayer's adjusted gross income. Thus, the Smiths can include $100 of these expenses in their itemized deductions [$800 minus (.02) $35,000)].

CHAPTER 10

DEPRECIATION, AMORTIZATION, AND DEPLETION

10.1 Depreciation

Depreciation is a deduction permitted to taxpayers to compensate them for the reasonable wear, tear, and obsolescence of certain assets used in a trade or business or held for the production of income. In order to be eligible, the following criteria must generally be satisfied:

1) The taxpayer must have an economic interest in the asset. An economic interest is said to exist if the value of the taxpayer's interest in the asset will be negatively affected by a decline in the value of the asset. Typically, an economic interest is indicated by the taxpayer having an ownership in the asset.

2) The asset must be tangible. An asset is tangible if it can be felt or touched and does not represent an interest in something else.

3) The asset must have a determinable useful life. A determinable useful life exists if, after a determinable period of time, the asset will cease to function or become obsolete.

4) The asset must have a determinable basis. The determination

of basis is critical in this regard because depreciation is computed based upon the taxpayer's basis in the asset.

5) The asset must be held for use in a trade or business or for the production of rental income.

6) The asset's useful life must exceed one year.

7) The asset must have been placed in service. To be considered placed in service the asset must be in a state of readiness capable of use for the purpose intended.

10.2 Accelerated Cost Recovery System

The rules governing the computation of depreciation have undergone change during the 1980s. The method used to compute depreciation depends upon when the asset was placed in service. The depreciation of assets placed in service after 1980 and before 1987 is determined under the accelerated cost recovery system (ACRS). Different rules govern the computation of personal property and real property under ACRS.

10.2.1 Personal Property

To compute depreciation of personal property, the class life into which the asset falls must be determined. Depending upon the class life into which an asset falls, different percentages must be multiplied by the cost of the asset to calculate the depreciation on the asset.

If a taxpayer desired, the taxpayer could elect out of using the regular method for computing depreciation of personal property under ACRS and compute depreciation under the straight-line method. The periods over which an asset could be depreciated under the straight-line method for assets of a given class life are:

For 3-year property — 3, 5, or 12 years
For 5-year property — 5, 12, or 25 years
For 10-year property — 10, 25, or 35 years
For 15-year public utility property — 15, 35, or 45 years

10.2.2 Real Estate

The depreciation of real estate under the Accelerated Cost Recovery System differs from the depreciation method used to compute that for personal property. Unlike depreciation for personal property, depreciation for real estate depends upon what month the asset was placed in service. In addition, depreciation is permitted on real estate for the year in which the real estate was disposed of, based upon the portion of the year that the real estate was in service by the taxpayer. In contrast, no depreciation is permitted for personal property placed in service under the ACRS regime for the year the property was disposed of. Under ACRS, tables are prescribed to determine depreciation of real estate, and alternative tables using straight-line are available should the taxpayer elect out of using the prescribed method. The class lives for determining depreciation for real estate are:

1) 15 years for real property placed in service after 1981 and before March 16, 1984. Alternative periods for depreciation are 15, 35, or 45 years.

2) 18 years for real property placed in service after March 15, 1984 and before May 9, 1985. Alternative periods for depreciation are 18, 35, or 45 years.

3) 19 years for real property placed in service after May 8, 1985 and before January 1, 1987. Alternative periods for depreciation are 19, 35, or 45 years.

10.3 ACRS "Section 179" Expense

Pursuant to Section 179, with regard to depreciable personal property placed in service after 1980 and before 1987, taxpayers could elect to expense and deduct $5,000 ($2,500 for a taxpayer married filing separately) of the cost in the first year the asset was placed in service. This amount constituted a reduction in the basis of the asset that was taken into account before depreciation on the asset was computed.

10.4 Modified Accelerated Cost Recovery System (MACRS)

Property placed in service after 1986 is depreciated under the Modified Cost Recovery System (MACRS).

10.5 Personal Property Under MACRS

Under MACRS a form of double declining balance method is to be used to depreciate personal property and 50% of the depreciation for the year of disposition is allowed (unless an excess amount of depreciable property held by the taxpayer is disposed of during the last quarter of the taxable year).

Under MACRS the class life of certain assets were changed. A table that can be used to determine the annual amount of depreciation for personal property based upon its class life is provided on the next page. Instead of using the regular MACRS percentages reflected in the table taxpayers can elect to depreciate certain assets over an alternative period using the straight-line method.

10.6 Real Estate Under MACRS

Drastic change was made in the period of depreciation for real estate under MACRS. Under MACRS depreciable residential real property is to be depreciated over 27.5 years using the straight-line method, and depreciable nonresidential real property is to be depreciated over 31.5 years using the straight-line method. Depreciation for both the year the asset is placed in service and disposed of is to be determined based upon the month of the year the asset is placed in service. In making this computation it is assumed that the asset has been placed in service in the middle of the month that the asset was placed in service and disposed of. As an alternative to using regular MACRS a taxpayer can elect to depreciate depreciable real estate (whether it is residential or nonresidential real estate) over a 40-year period using the straight-line method. In applying such an alternative, a mid-month convention applies for both the year the property is placed in service and disposed of.

If the Recovery Year is:	and the Recovery Period is:					
	3-year	5-year	7-year	10-year	15-year	20-year
		the Depreciation Rate is:				
1	33.33	20.00	14.29	10.00	5.00	3.750
2	44.45	32.00	24.49	18.00	9.50	7.219
3	14.81	19.20	17.49	14.40	8.55	6.677
4	7.41	11.52	12.49	11.52	7.70	6.177
5		11.52	8.93	9.22	6.93	5.713
6		5.76	8.92	7.37	6.23	5.285
7			8.93	6.55	5.90	4.888
8			4.46	6.55	5.90	4.522
9				6.56	5.91	4.462
10				6.55	5.90	4.461
11				3.28	5.91	4.462
12					5.90	4.461
13					5.91	4.462
14					5.90	4.461
15					5.91	4.462
16					2.95	4.461
17						4.462
18						4.461
19						4.462
20						4.461
21						2.231

10.7 Section 179 Under MACRS

For depreciable personal property placed in service, the "Section 179" expense that could be elected for the first year that the asset was placed in service was increased to $10,000 ($5,000 for taxpayers married filing separately). This amount must be reduced if:

1) The cost of the "Section 179" qualifying property placed in service is less than the $10,000 maximum amount, in

which case the maximum "179" expense is limited to the amount of "Section 179" qualifying property placed in service during the year. Note this limit also was applied to "179" expense with regard to property placed in service under the ACRS regime.

2) If the taxable income of the taxpayer in the trade or business in which the "Section 179" property is placed is less than the maximum amount of "Section 179" expense otherwise allowed, the maximum of Section 179 expense is limited to the amount of the amount of taxable income produced in the trade or business. Note that the taxable income of relevance in this regard is that before taking into account the "Section 179" expense.

3) Where the "Section 179" expense qualifying property placed in service by the taxpayer during the year exceeds $200,000, the taxpayer must reduce the maximum "Section 179" expense otherwise permitted by the number of dollars of "Section 179" expense qualifying property placed in service in excess of $200,000.

10.8 Amortization

Amortization rather than depreciation is what is generally used as a means to recover the cost of intangible assets used in the taxpayer's trade or business with a determinable life. Unlike depreciation, amortization can only be taken on a straight-line basis over the amortization period.

Expenditures for which amortization is permitted include:

1) **Business Start-up Expenses**—These are expenses that would be deductible if incurred in an existing trade or business but are incurred prior to the start of such trade or business are amortizable over 60 months.

2) **Certified Pollution Control Facilities**—These are generally amortizable over a 60-month period.

3) **Research and Experimental Expenditures**—Taxpayers generally have an option to either take a current deduction or amortize over 60 months research and experimental expenditures incurred in connection with their trade or business. However, most taxpayers choose to write off research and experimental expenditures immediately, in the year when these expenses are incurred.

10.9 Depletion

A deduction is allowed for depletion. Depletion is a means of recovering the cost of wasting natural resources, e.g., minerals, oil, and gas.

There exist two principal methods of computing depletion for tax purposes:

1) **Cost Method**—Used to determine depletion based upon an amount of depletion per unit of production.

2) **Percentage Depletion**—In contrast to cost depletion, percentage depletion involves computing depletion by multiplying a designated percentage by the gross income from the asset. For instance, oil wells have a depletion deduction derived by multiplying 15% times the gross income from the property. Different percentages are prescribed for different types of property. Unlike cost depletion, you may claim percentage depletion even though your basis in the property has been reduced to zero.

Review Questions

1. Distinguish between depreciation, amortization, and depletion.

Depreciation is a means of recovering the cost of a tangible asset over time due to the reasonable wear and tear or obsolescence of such asset. Amortization, meanwhile, is an analogous process by which the cost of an intangible asset with a determinable useful life in excess of one year can be recovered, and depletion is a means of recovering the cost of wasting natural resources.

2. *What criteria must generally be satisfied in order to depreciate an asset?*

Generally, the asset must be tangible and must have a determinable useful life in excess of one year. The taxpayer must have an economic interest in the asset, a basis must exist in the asset, and the asset must have been placed in service in order to be depreciable.

3. *What is the importance of "placed in service" in determining depreciation?*

An asset cannot be depreciated until it has been placed in service, that is, in use by the business. In addition, when the asset was placed in service governs the depreciation system applicable to depreciating the asset.

4. *What are ACRS and MACRS?*

ACRS, which stands for accelerated cost recovery system, is the system governing the computation of depreciation on assets placed in service after 1980 and before 1987. MACRS, which stands for the modified accelerated cost recovery system, is applicable for the computation of depreciation of assets placed in service after 1986.

5. *What is "Section 179" expense?*

"Section 179" expense may generally be elected with regard to depreciable tangible property placed in service after 1980, for the first year the asset has been placed in service. The Section 179 expense constitutes a deduction analogous to rapid depreciation.

6. *How does taking "Section 179" expense affect the computation of depreciation?*

The amount of "Section 179" expense taken constitutes a down-

ward adjustment of basis in the asset which must be taken into account prior to computing depreciation on the asset in the following years.

7. *Over how many years must business start-up expenses be amortized?*

Business start-up expenses are amortizable over a 60-month period.

8. *What are the two types of depletion?*

The two types of depletion are cost depletion and percentage depletion.

CHAPTER 11

SPECIAL LOSS RULES

11.1 Losses

As a general rule, a loss realized on the disposition of a business asset is deductible toward adjusted gross income. In certain instances, the amount of a loss that is deductible may be subject to a limitation. For example, a loss on the sale of personal use property is not deductible nor is a loss on a like-kind exchange.

11.2 Casualty and Theft Losses

A casualty or theft loss on property used in the taxpayer's trade or business, or on property held for investment purposes is generally deductible toward adjusted gross income. The amount of such loss is computed as follows:

1) **In the case of a complete destruction or theft**—The adjusted basis of the asset minus insurance or other amounts that can be claimed as reimbursement.

2) **Where there is but a partial destruction or theft**—The lesser of the decrease in the fair market value of the asset or its adjusted basis minus amounts received as insurance or otherwise as reimbursement.

Where the casualty or theft occurs to personal-use property, the ability to obtain a deduction is more difficult. This results due to additional amounts that must be subtracted out in determining the amount of the loss and the treatment of any such loss as an itemized deduction.

In computing the amount of a casualty or theft loss on personal-use property (regardless of whether there is a complete or partial destruction or a theft) the following steps are undertaken:

1) The lesser of the decrease in fair market value or adjusted basis of the property

2) Minus any reimbursement (other than that for increased living expenses)

3) Minus $100 for each separate casualty or theft event

4) Minus 10% of the taxpayer's adjusted gross income

EXAMPLE

Bob's home was destroyed in a hurricane. The adjusted basis of the house was $30,000 and the decrease in fair market value caused by the event was $20,000. Bob's AGI for the year was $50,000. Bob received no insurance as a result of the casualty. Bob can include $14,900 in his itemized deductions as a result of the casualty. This equals $20,000 minus $100 and 10% of his adjusted gross income.

Normally, a casualty deduction will be taken on the tax return for the year in which the casualty occurred. Where, however, the casualty occurs in an event causing the area to be declared a national disaster area, the casualty can be claimed on a amended return for the tax year prior to that in which the event occurred.

11.3 Related Party Transactions

Where property is sold at a loss to a related party, a loss realized cannot be recognized as a tax deduction. The loss realized but not recognized may still have an effect upon a subsequent sale by the related party purchaser to an unrelated party.

On a subsequent sale to an unrelated party, if the asset is sold for more than the original related party's sales price, gain will be computed by using the original related party seller's basis as that of the related purchaser. If the sales price is less than that paid by the related party purchaser, then the purchase price paid by the related purchaser will be used as the basis for computing loss. Should the sales price fall within the range of the original related party seller's basis and the lower amount paid by the related party purchaser neither gain nor loss will be recognized.

11.4 Gambling Losses

Gambling losses generally constitute a type of itemized deduction. Such are only allowed as an itemized deduction to the extent of the taxpayer's gambling winnings.

11.5 Worthless Stocks and Bonds

The tax law permits taxpayers to deduct a loss to the extent of their investment for worthless stocks or bonds, e.g., when the company has gone bankrupt. Such loss is generally a capital loss. In determining whether the loss is a long-term or short-term capital loss, the stock or bond is considered to have become worthless on the last day of the taxable year in which worthlessness occurred.

11.6 Sham Sales

A sham sale is a transaction lacking any economic substance and merely undergone to generate a deductible loss for tax purposes. If a transaction is found to be a sham, any loss on the transaction will generally be disallowed.

11.7 Wash Sales

A wash sale exists if stocks, securities, or stock options are sold at a loss and within 30 days before or after the sale producing the loss substantially identical stocks, securities, or stock options are

purchased. Substantially identical for this purpose involves a similar interest in the same corporation in the same class of stock sold.

A loss realized on a wash sale will be disallowed to the extent the number of shares, securities, or options sold are covered by substantially similar interests acquired within the 30 day before or after period.

EXAMPLE

Z sold 1,000 shares of Cobra Corporation class A common stock resulting in a $2,000 loss realized. Within 15 days of the sale Z purchased 500 shares of substantially the same stock in Cobra. As a result of the purchase, Z can only recognize $1,000 (50%) of the $2,000 loss realized.

11.8 Hobby Losses

Generally expenses related to a hobby can only be deducted to the extent of income from the hobby activity, and then only as a type of itemized deduction. This treatment differs from that of an expense incurred by a taxpayer from a trade or business expense. Whether an activity will be classified as a hobby or a trade or business largely depends upon whether the activity was conducted with a good faith intent to produce a profit. If the activity was so conducted, generally trade or business status will result; if not, hobby status will be accorded. The tax law provides a presumption in this regard. Generally if the activity produces a profit in three of five years, a profit intent will be found; for horse breeding, training, and racing, a two-out-of-seven-year period rule applies.

11.9 Converted Property

Where property is converted from personal use to depreciable use, depreciation is to be computed based upon the lesser of the adjusted basis of the property on the date of conversion or the fair market value of the property on the date of conversion. When the property is later sold to determine gain or loss, the following rules apply:

1) Generally use the adjusted basis of the property on the date of conversion less depreciation as the basis to compute gain or loss.

2) If the asset is sold for less than the adjusted basis on the date of conversion less depreciation, should the fair market value of the property on the date of conversion less depreciation be lower, use it as the basis for computing loss. If the fair market value of the asset less depreciation is lower than the adjusted basis on the date of conversion less depreciation, and the sales price is more than the fair market value less depreciation but less than the adjusted basis less depreciation, neither gain nor loss will be recognized for tax purposes.

11.10 Net Operating Losses

To the extent a taxpayer has losses from trade or business operations exceeding all trade or business income, such loss is referred to as a net operating loss. A net operating loss must generally be carried back three years and forward 15 years. Taxpayers can elect out of the carryback period in which case the net operating loss need only be carried forward. A net operating loss is used to offset taxable income in the years to which it is carried.

Review Questions

1. What is a loss for tax purposes?

A loss is generally computed on a sale or exchange of property and equals the amount by which the adjusted basis of the asset disposed of exceeds the amount realized on the disposition. Generally a loss realized on a disposition of property is also recognized, however exceptions to such recognition exist, e.g., for losses realized on the disposition of personal-use property and gains and losses realized on a like-kind exchange.

2. *During the year the copy machine owned and used by the tax-payer for his business was stolen. The machine had a basis of $5,000 and a fair market value of $7,000 at the time of the theft. The taxpayer recovered $2,000 of insurance reimbursement as a result of the theft. How should the taxpayer treat the theft for tax purposes?*

The taxpayer may deduct $3,000 ($5,000 minus $2,000) toward adjusted gross income for tax purposes as a result of the theft.

3. *Assume the same facts as above except that the machine was held for the taxpayer's personal use, and the taxpayer had an adjusted gross income of $25,000 for the year. How would the taxpayer treat the theft under these circumstances?*

Under these facts the taxpayer will be entitled to an itemized deduction of $400 as a result of the theft ($5,000 minus [$2,000 plus $100 plus 10%($25,000)] of personal use property.

4. *Jim sold stock in which he had a basis of $10,000 to his son for $7,000. How much of the loss on the sale can Jim deduct?*

Jim cannot recognize and deduct any of the $3,000 loss realized due to the sale being to a related party.

5. *In November, Sam, a calendar-year taxpayer, invested $10,000 in X Corporation common stock. In January of the following tax year the stock became worthless. What is the tax consequence of the worthlessness of the stock to Sam for tax purposes?*

Sam is entitled to a $10,000 long-term capital loss in the following tax year as a result of the stock becoming worthless. Although the stock was only held by Sam for three months, the tax law considers the stock to have become worthless on the last day of the taxable year in which worthlessness occurred in determining the taxpayer's holding period in it.

6. *Bill converted his residence entirely into rental property. At the time of the conversion Bill had a basis in the home of $70,000*

and the fair market value of the home was $65,000. On what amount will Bill compute depreciation for tax purposes?

Bill is required to compute depreciation on $65,000 as this is the lesser of fair market value of the property on the date of conversion and the adjusted basis on such date.

CHAPTER 12

CREDITS

12.1 What is a Credit?

A credit is a subtraction from tax. In computing the amount of tax that must be paid the government, or the amount of refund, or the amount of credit against future taxes to which the taxpayer is entitled, taxpayers should subtract credits from their tax liability. A credit is preferable to a deduction in that a credit can offset a taxpayer's tax liability dollar for dollar, whereas a deduction can only produce a tax savings equal to the taxpayer's marginal tax rate multiplied by the amount of the deduction.

12.2 Earned Income Credit

To qualify for the earned income credit, the taxpayers must either be:

1) Married and entitled to claim a dependency exemption for their child or stepchild;

2) A surviving spouse;

3) A custodial parent even though such may have agreed to allow the noncustodial spouse to claim the dependency exemption; or

4) Head of household meeting the general criteria with a child or stepchild.

The IRS prescribes a table by which the earned income credit can be computed. Generally in using the table the taxpayer need only ascertain the amount of the credit corresponding to the taxpayer's earned income. Should the taxpayer's adjusted gross income exceed a prescribed amount, the taxpayer must determine the credit corresponding to such adjusted gross income figure and compare that to the credit corresponding to the taxpayer's earned income and use the lesser of the two credit amounts as the earned income credit. The taxpayers can get a refund of the credit even if they don't owe any tax.

12.3 Credit for the Elderly or Permanently Disabled

To qualify for this credit the taxpayer must be 65 years of age or older or permanently disabled. If the credit is qualified for, it is computed using the following steps:

Credit Base
−   Social security benefits received, railroad retirements received, nontaxable pensions received, and 50% of excess adjusted gross income

---

Balance
× by 15%

Tentative Credit

The credit amount allowed a taxpayer is the lesser of the tentative credit or the taxpayer's tax liability. In making the above computation for 1991, the credit base is:

$7,500 for married filing jointly should both spouses qualify

$5,000 for married filing jointly should one spouse qualify, head of household, and single

84

$3,750 for married filing separately

Excess adjusted gross income for 1991 is AGI in excess of $10,000 for married filing jointly, $7,500 for single taxpayers, and $5,000 for married filing separately.

12.4 Child Care and Disabled Dependent Credit

This credit is allowed for expenses incurred with regard to a child of the taxpayer under the age of 13 and a disabled dependent of the taxpayer to enable the taxpayer to be employed. Generally the credit is computed by multiplying what is referred to as the applicable percentage by the lesser of the amount expended to have the qualified individual(s) watched over or a prescribed dollar amount. Amounts paid to someone whom the taxpayer can claim as a dependent will not be included in the credit computation.

12.5 Low-Income-Housing Credit

Set to expire at the end of 1991, but likely to be extended, the low-income-housing credit was established to stimulate the establishment of an increased number of affordable low income housing. Unlike most credits the low income housing credit is a credit amount that can be taken each year for up to a ten-year period. An annual credit of approximately 9% is available for newly constructed low income housing and approximately 4% for existing structures converted into low income housing and Federally subsidized low income housing.

12.6 Rehabilitation Credit

This credit is available for the rehabilitation of certain types of structures. For certified historic structures a credit of 20% of the rehabilitation costs can be taken as a credit; a credit percentage of 10% is available for nonhistoric structures placed in service before 1936. In order to utilize this credit, the tax law requires that the taxpayer depreciate the building using the straight-line method. Costs of enlarging or improving the structure do not qualify as rehabilitation costs for this purpose.

12.7 Recapture of Credits

The tax law generally provides that should property on which a credit was taken be disposed of in a taxable sale or exchange or have its trade or business use fall beneath 50% within a designated period of time, at least some of the credit taken must be recaptured. The recapture of a credit operates differently than the recapture of depreciation. Unlike depreciation recapture, the amount of credit recaptured is added on to the taxpayer's tax liability for the year of recapture and is determined based upon the period of time separating the placement of the asset in service and the recapture event independent of whether there is any gain on the event.

Review Questions

1. Why is a tax credit preferable to a deduction?

Because a credit can offset a taxpayer's tax liability dollar for dollar; whereas a deduction only produces a tax savings benefit equal to the taxpayer's marginal tax rate multiplied by the amount of the deduction.

2. What is the base amount used in computing the credit for the elderly and permanently disabled for a husband and wife filing a joint return where the husband is 70 and the wife 67 years of age?

The base amount for married filing jointly where both spouses qualify as either elderly or permanently disabled is $7,500.

3. What is the objective of the child care and disabled dependent credit?

The objective is to help families to afford care for their children and disabled dependents to enable the taxpayer to hold full-time employment.

4. *How does recapture of a credit affect a taxpayer's tax liability?*

   The amount of credit recaptured must be added directly onto the taxpayer's tax liability for the year of recapture.

CHAPTER 13

ALTERNATIVE MINIMUM TAX

13.1 What is the Alternative Minimum Tax (AMT)?

The alternative minimum tax is a special additional tax imposed upon a taxpayer's regular tax if the taxpayer's tentative minimum tax (computed using the steps in 13.2) exceeds the taxpayer's regular tax. An alternative minimum tax computation exists for both individuals and corporations. The primary purpose underlying the existence of the alternative minimum tax is one of equity. In this regard the AMT largely exists to prevent taxpayers with significant amounts of economic wealth from incurring little or no taxes.

13.2 Structure of the Computation

In computing the alternative minimum tax, the following steps are utilized:

1) Taxable income of the taxpayer (this can be derived from the taxpayer's regular tax return).

2) Plus (or minus) certain adjustments.

3) Plus tax preferences.

4) The aggregate of steps 1, 2, and 3 constitute the taxpayer's alternative minimum taxable income (AMTI).

5) Subtract the taxpayer's exemption amount for AMT purposes from the AMTI.

6) Multiply the total after step 5 by the alternative minimum tax rate. For 1990 this rate is 21%, and for 1991, 24%.

7) Subtract allowable credits for AMT purposes from the product calculated in step 6, the difference is the taxpayer's tentative minimum tax.

8) Subtract the taxpayer's regular tax (from the taxpayer's regular tax return) from the tentative minimum tax. Should the tentative minimum tax exceed the taxpayer's regular tax the excess is the taxpayer's AMT. Should however the taxpayer's tentative minimum tax not exceed the taxpayer's regular tax, no alternative minimum tax will be owed.

13.3 Adjustments

There exist a large number of different types of adjustments, some of the more commonly encountered include:

Adjustments Upward

Add:

1) Standard deduction if utilized.

2) Total exemption amount taken on regular return.

3) Itemized deduction if itemizing on the regular return.

4) Depreciation taken above that allowed under the straight-line method for assets placed in service after 1986.

5) Amounts that would be included for the year if percentage of completion method were used on long-term contracts if completed contract is being used.

6) Special computation to determine how much, if any, passive losses taken on regular return can be used.

Subtract:

Certain itemized deductions can be subtracted. These include:

1) Medical expenses, but only to the extent exceeding 10% of the taxpayer's adjusted gross income.

2) Home mortgage interest.

3) Investment interest expense, but only to the extent of net investment income for the tax year.

13.4 Preferences

Unlike adjustments, preferences can only be an addition to the taxpayer's regular taxable income in computing the alternative minimum tax.

Preference items include:

1) Charitable contributions taken on the donation of appreciated property to the extent the amount of the charitable contribution exceeds the basis of the property contributed.

2) Tax exempt interest on certain private activity bonds.

3) Accelerated depreciation taken in excess of straight-line on assets placed in service before 1987.

4) Percentage depletion deducted to the extent exceeding the taxpayer's investment in oil, gas, and geothermal properties.

5) Excess of intangible drilling costs taken above a prescribed percentage.

Review Questions

1. What is the alternative minimum tax?

The alternative minimum tax is essentially the minimum tax a taxpayer has to pay. When the alternative minimum tax exceeds the taxpayer's regular tax, the taxpayer must pay the difference as the alternative minimum tax. The alternative minimum tax exists in order to ensure that taxpayers with a large amount of economic income pay an equitable amount of tax.

2. *What are the basic steps undergone in computing the alternative minimum tax?*

Regular taxable income plus (minus) adjustments plus tax preferences minus the taxpayer's alternative minimum tax exemption amount equals alternative minimum taxable income. Multiply alternative minimum taxable income by the applicable alternative minimum tax rate and subtract allowable credits and the taxpayer's regular tax. Any excess is the taxpayer's alternative minimum tax.

CHAPTER 14

TAX ACCOUNTING

14.1 The Annual Accounting Period Concept— What is It?

Taxpayers file returns on an annual basis. Each return generally reflects the financial transactions of tax significance undergone by the taxpayer within an annual period. The use of these typical 12-month intervals as the basis for determining taxpayers' tax is referred to as the annual accounting period concept.

14.2 The Tax Year

Most individuals utilize a calendar taxable year. A calendar tax year is one covering the 12-month period of January 1–December 31. If the taxpayer does not maintain regular books and records, use of a calendar tax year is required.

A fiscal tax year may be elected by new taxpayers who regularly keep their books and records on such basis. A fiscal tax year is a tax year of 52–53 weeks which generally ends on the same day of the same month each year (other than December 31).

Taxpayers who are sole proprietors must use the same tax year for reporting their income from the sole proprietorship as their regular personal income.

14.3 Methods of Accounting

An accounting method is the rules regularly used by a taxpayer to determine how and when income or expense will be reported.

The tax law provides for use of reasonable accounting methods. The primary methods used, however, are:

1) Cash Method

2) Accrual Method

3) Hybrid Method

Most individuals use the cash method. The accrual method is mandatory for operations involving inventories. In some instances a taxpayer may use a hybrid method, which involves treating some items on the cash method and others on the accrual method.

14.4 Cash Method

Inclusions in Income—Cash-method taxpayers must include an item of income in their gross income when the item is actually or constructively received. Actual receipt occurs when the taxpayer takes physical delivery of the item of income, e.g., is paid wages. Constructive receipt takes place when the item of income is available to be physically received at the taxpayer's discretion without any substantial restriction, e.g., interest on a checking account.

Expenses—No deduction or credit is generally permitted to a cash-method taxpayer until the item is actually paid. Note exceptions to this rule exist, e.g., depreciation.

14.5 Accrual Accounting

Inclusions in Income—An accrual-method taxpayer will include an item in income when the "all events test" is satisfied. According to the all-events test, this occurs when:

1) The right to receive income is fixed.

2) The amount to be received is reasonably determinable.

Expenses—In order to take a deduction, an accrual-method taxpayer must generally meet the following criteria:

1) The liability must be certain.

2) The amount of the liability must be reasonably determinable.

3) Economic performance must have been received.

14.6 Special Rules

14.6.1 Prepaid Expenses

Generally, neither a cash nor accrual method taxpayer can accelerate deductions by prepaying expenses that would cover a period beyond the current one. Instead, prepaid expenses must typically be deducted pro rata over the period covered.

14.6.2 Prepaid Income

Generally, whether the taxpayer is on the cash or accrual method, if the taxpayer receives income in advance of earning it, such income must be included in the taxpayer's income in the year of receipt. Exceptions exist for accrual-method taxpayers in the following situations:

1) If the taxpayer receives a payment for services which will be completed in the following tax year, the taxpayer can defer reporting such in income until such following taxable year.

2) If the taxpayer is an accrual-method membership organization without capital stock, the organization can report membership fees received over the lesser of the membership period or 36 months.

3) Subscription fees received can be reported in income over the subscription period.

14.6.3 Contested Items

When a taxpayer contests liability for an item that would be deductible, e.g., state income taxes, the taxpayer will be permitted a deduction if paying the item to the claimant, the court, or an agreed upon independent party and seeking a refund. Should the matter be resolved and the taxpayer found to owe less than that which the taxpayer took as a deduction, the amount of the anticipated refund will be included in the taxpayer's gross income under the tax benefit rule. If the taxpayer is a cash-method taxpayer, such inclusion will result when the refund is actually or constructively received.

14.6.4 Claim-of-Right Doctrine

If a taxpayer erroneously receives income in a year, such income must be reported in the year of receipt. In the year the taxpayer repays the erroneously received amount, the taxpayer will obtain a deduction for the amount repaid. Should the amount repaid exceed $3,000, the taxpayer can either take a deduction for the amount repaid for the year of repayment or compute the deduction based on the tax rates to which the taxpayer was subject in the year the item was erroneously received.

14.6.5 Credit Cards

When medical expenses or charitable contributions are charged to a taxpayer's credit card, the taxpayer may take a deduction on his return for the year of the charge rather than the year in which the amount charged is actually paid.

14.7 Installment Sale

As a general rule, taxpayers must recognize gain or loss on a sale in the year of the sale. The tax law provides taxpayers with a break by allowing gain recognized on an installment sale to be reported over time as payments on the sale are received. To qualify as an installment sale, the seller must not be a dealer in the property sold, the sale must be for a gain recognized, and at least one payment sales price must be received in a year after that in which the sale takes place. If these criteria are met, the installment rules automatically apply. If the taxpayer does not want these rules to apply, the taxpayer must make an election not to have the installment rules apply.

14.7.1 Computation of Gain

Any amounts received as interest are included in gross income in the year received. A portion of each payment of sales price received on an installment will be included in the taxpayer's gross income. The amount so included is determined by multiplying the amount received by the taxpayer's gross profit percentage. The taxpayer's gross profit percentage (also referred to as the gross profit ratio) is generally equal to:

Sales price minus (adjusted basis plus selling expenses plus depreciation recaptured) divided by sales price

It should be noted that in computing the gross profit percentage any depreciation recaptured on the sale is to be taken into income in the year of the sale and reflected in the numerator. The denominator, while usually equal to the sales price, must be modified where the seller is relieved of a liability on the sale or the sale is linked to a like-kind exchange. Where the seller is relieved of a liability on the sale, the lesser of the liability relief or adjusted basis of the property sold is subtracted from the selling price in computing the denominator. Where the sale is connected to a like-kind exchange, the fair market value of the like-kind property received is subtracted from the selling price in computing the denominator.

The denominator of the gross profit ratio is typically referred to as the contract price.

EXAMPLE

Bill sells real estate in which he has a basis of $40,000 for $100,000 (excluding interest). Twenty-thousand dollars of the selling price is to be received each year for a five-year period. Bill's gross profit ratio on the sale is 60%, and 60% of each payment of sales price received will be included in his gross income.

14.8 At Risk Rules

Taxpayers are only permitted to take loss deductions from investment activities to the extent they are considered to be at risk in the activity. The amount deemed to be at risk is generally the amount of funds, adjusted basis of property contributed to the activity, and liabilities related to the activity for which the taxpayer can be held personally liable. The amount at risk will increase or decrease each year as more amounts are contributed to the activity or losses are taken with regard to the activity.

14.9 Passive Activity Loss Limitation Rules

Generally a taxpayer is only permitted to utilize deductions attributable to an investment in passive activities to the extent of the taxpayer's aggregate income from such activities. Excess deductions must be carried forward and used to offset excess passive activity income in subsequent taxable years. When a passive activity is disposed of in a taxable sale or exchange, any carried-forward losses related to the activity may be used in full. Passive activities for purposes of the above rules include:

1) A trade or business in which the taxpayer has an interest but does not materially participate.

2) Rental activities.

14.10 Inventory

In computing cost of goods sold and ending inventory, taxpayers may use such methods as first-in-first-out, last-in-first-out, and lower cost or market. Due to changes made in the tax law, there has been an increase in the types of costs which must be included in inventory.

Review Questions

1. *Most individuals utilize what type of tax year?*

   Most individual taxpayers utilize a calendar tax year.

2. *In 1991 a physician, an accrual-method taxpayer, performed an operation on a patient for which the patient was billed $500 as agreed upon. Payment was not received by the physician until 1992. In what year will the physician have to report the $500 as gross income.*

   The physician must include the $500 in gross income in 1991, as this is the year in which the all-events test was satisfied and the physician is an accrual-method taxpayer.

3. *When must a cash-method taxpayer include an amount in gross income?*

   A cash-method taxpayer must include an item in gross income (which constitutes an element of gross income) in the year such item is actually or constructively received.

4. *An accountant pays $5,000 for the next five years rent on January 1, 1991. How much can the accountant deduct for 1991 as rental expense?*

   Prepaid expenses covering a period in excess of 12 months must be prorated over the period covered. Here the taxpayer can deduct $1,000 (one-fifth of the prepaid rent) for 1991.

5. *Joe, an engineer, sells land which he has held for several years for $100,000. Joe's basis in the land is $20,000. Of the $100,000 sales price, $20,000 will be paid each year for five years. Does the sale qualify for installment sale treatment?*

   Yes, the sale qualifies for installment sale treatment as the taxpayer is not a dealer in the property sold, the property has been sold for a gain which will have to be recognized, and at least one payment of the sales price will be received in a year after that in which the sale took place.

6. *John sells land, which he has held for investment for 5 years. The sales price is $200,000, of which $40,000 will be paid in the year of the sale, and $10,000 will be paid in each of the 10 years following the year of the sale. Sixty-thousand dollars of the sales price is composed of a mortgage on the property which the buyer will assume. John's basis in the property is $100,000. How much of the $40,000 cash received in the year of the sale must be included in John's gross income?*

John's gross profit percentage is 71.43%, this gross profit percentage is derived by dividing the gross profit on the sale of $100,000 ($200,000 minus $100,000) by the contract price of $140,000 ($200,000 minus $60,000 mortgage relief). As a result, $28,572 ($40,000 multiplied by 71.43%) of gain on the sale must be recognized in the year of the sale.

7. *What are the at-risk rules?*

The at-risk rules generally limit a taxpayer's ability to take deductions and credits from an investment activity to the amount the taxpayer is considered to be at risk in the activity.

CHAPTER 15

RECENT CHANGES IN THE INCOME TAX LAW

Both Congress and the courts cause changes in the income tax law. Following are recent changes:

15.1 Inflation Adjustments

Prices continue to rise each year. This is **inflation**. So almost every year Congress revises both dollar amounts and tax rates (percentages) in income tax law. This is then called **inflation adjustments**. Some of the major changes are as follows:

(a) The personal and dependent exemption amount

(b) The standard deduction

(c) The adjusted gross income thresholds for phaseout of personal exemption amounts.

(d) The adjusted gross income thresholds for limitation of some itemized deductions

(e) Income tax brackets for various tax rates

(f) Depreciation limits on business-use vehicles. (Over the years these levels have become more generous, or larger. They have been indexed, or revised for inflation.)

(g) Standard mileage allowance for business-use vehicles. (The deductible rate for business mileage driven has been gradually increased over recent years.)

(h) Wage ceiling for social security taxes has been raised.

(i) Modified Adjusted Gross Income phaseout thresholds for exclusion of interest from Series EE Bonds has been revised.

(j) Maximum income level at which the earned income credit is available has been changed.

(k) Revision of corporate tax rates

(l) Top estate and gift tax rates have been increased.

15.2 Donations of Appreciated Property

Donations of Appreciated Property are now deductible at fair market value, rather than at cost value. (Let us say we purchase common stock at $100 which gradually increases to $150, and then we give this to charity. We can make a charitable deduction of $150 if we itemize.)

15.3 Determining the Non-Taxable Portion of Each Payment from a Retirement Plan Distribution

(An annuity paid to retired people.) This is done originally by dividing the cost of the entire contract by the total number of periodic payments one expects to receive. If it is a life annuity, one determines the number of payments by an Internal Revenue Service actuarial table.

15.4 Kiddie Tax

For children under age 14 with Unearned Incomes. Tax thresholds change over the years, but parents or guardians must file returns for their children earning income above the threshold. The parent is also liable for the payment of the tax. (A parent may elect to include a child's income in the parent's return.)

15.5 Changes in Computation of the Alternative Minimum Tax

Rates and exemptions have been increased. The alternative minimum tax was set up to insure that no taxpayer with substantial income can avoid significant tax liability by using exclusions, deductions, and credits.

15.6 Social Security Changes

(a) Social security and medicare tax earnings bases have been increased.

(b) All people, including infants, now need social security numbers.

15.7 Cosmetic Surgery

Costs of cosmetic surgery, such as facelifts, are no longer deductible.

15.8 Personal Interest Payments

Personal interest payments, such as interest on loans to buy a personal-use car, are no longer deductible.

15.9 Investment Interest is now Deductible only to the Extent of Investment Income

If one borrows money to buy stocks, the interest expense on the loan is subtractable only from any income one earns from this investment.

15.10 Passive Losses are Deductible only to the Extent of Passive Income

A passive investment is one that takes only minimal or non-existent activity in earning the income—such as interest or dividend income.

15.11 Deduction of Tax Preparation Fees for Sole Proprietors, Farmers, and Landlords

These can now be deducted directly from income rather than on Schedule A as done previously.

15.12 Schedule C-EZ

This schedule is a short form for small business proprietors.

15.13 Extended Tax Tables

These tables now can be used by taxpayers with incomes up to $100,000.

15.14 Revised Withholding Tables for Employers

These extend tables up to $100,000 income for people using Form 1040.

15.15 Exclusion for Employer-Provided Education Assistance

Employees need not count as income the educational assistance provided by employers, up to a certain limit.

15.16 Work Opportunity Credit for Employers of Targeted Groups

Employers get a credit for hiring people from needy families with children, veterans, ex-felons, high-risk youth, people in vocational rehabilitation, summer youth employees, and people on supplemental social security.

15.17 Low-Income Housing Credit

This is given to people or firms for construction or rehabilitation of low-income housing in the year that it is placed in service.

15.18 Amortization of Goodwill or Going-Concern Value

These intangible assets used in valuing a business can now be written off over a shorter period than previously.

15.19 Safe Harbor for People Underpaying their Estimated Taxes

If people paying estimated tax pay an estimated tax of at least 90% of their tax liability for the current year, they will be able to avoid the penalty for underpayment.

15.20 Revision of Rules for Tip Income

Tipped employees might be audited if they don't sign a Tipped Employee Participation Agreement. Those who don't keep timely records are encouraged to sign.

15.21 Business Expense Deductions are Changed

Travelling business people's deductions for meals and entertainment of customers are revised periodically by Congress.

15.22 Debt Discharge Income Exclusion

(Debt Forgiveness is a type of income.) One may now choose to exclude income from the discharge of a debt secured by business real property to the extent that the principal amount of the debt immediately before the discharge exceeded the fair market value minus any other debt secured by the property.

15.23 Depreciation of Nonresidential Real Property

The length of time an owner now will use to depreciate this type has been increased to 39 years.

15.24 Presidential Election Campaign Fund

A taxpayer now is able to donate $3 to this fund each year.

15.25 Publicly Traded Securities

Individuals or corporations may now defer the gain on the sale of publicly-traded securities (such as stocks) if they use this money to finance small businesses of disadvantaged persons.

15.26 Capital Gains

Individuals may exclude from taxes 1/2 of capital gains realized on the sale of small business stock which they have held over five years.

15.27 Accuracy-Related Penalties

In order to avoid penalties for underpayment of taxes, the taxpayer must have at least a "reasonable basis" for his position.

15.28 Reporting Discharge of Indebtedness

(Forgiveness of Debt is considered income by the government.) Financial entities must file information returns with the Internal Revenue Service reporting any discharge of indebtedness of $600 or more.

15.29 Installment Payments

There have been changes in the rules by which taxpayers may legally make late payments of taxes to the Internal Revenue Service through installments.

15.30 Exclusion of Interest on EE Bonds

Interest on government Series EE bonds is tax-free if they are used to build a college fund. (For instance, parents saving money for future college tuition of growing children.) However this exclusion is phased out for higher-income taxpayers.

15.31 Real Estate Professionals

If more than half the personal services that a taxpayer performs are in real property trades or businesses, these are not subject to passive-loss rules. (Passive-loss rules require passive losses to be deducted only from passive income such as dividends and interest.) Thus these realtors would be able to deduct losses from any form of income.

15.32 Charitable Contributions

(a) Taxpayer must have written substantiation from donee organization for a contribution of $250 or more.

(b) Mileage allowance for volunteers working for charitable organizations has increased from 12 cents per mile to 14 cents per mile.

15.33 Moving Expenses

Taxpayers deducting for moving expenses must have moved 50 miles or more, have full-time work at the new location, have worked at least 39 weeks at the previous location. Also, moving expenses must be closely related to the date when new work is begun. There are no longer any deductions for house-hunting trips.

15.34 Club Dues

Club membership dues are no longer deductible.

15.35 Social Security Benefits

Some of the social security benefits are now taxable to higher-income recipients.

15.36 Empowerment Zones

Business people who have businesses in government-designated Empowerment Zones get faster depreciation rates and alternative minimum tax credits. This is to encourage business investment in depressed areas.

15.37 Indian Reservations

Business people on Indian reservations may depreciate assets at an increased rate. They also get a tax credit for hiring tribal members whose wages do not exceed $30,000.

15.38 Health Insurance for Self-Employed People

The deduction for this is made permanent and increased to 30% of one's health costs.

15.39 Earned Income Credit Changes

(a) A person can no longer claim Earned Income Credit if he has more than $2,200 in dividends, interest, or capital gains. Adjusted gross income must be increased by the amount of any net capital loss.

(b) If a person has filed a fraudulent or reckless return, there will be a long waiting period before he can claim this credit again.

(c) Military people outside the United States are now treated as if they lived in the United States. They can now receive Earned Income Credit.

(d) Prisoners can no longer receive Earned Income Credit.

(e) Non-Resident Aliens cannot receive Earned Income Credit.

(f) The credit is expanded to a higher rate for one child. Also there is more credit for 2 or more children. The maximum income for which the credit is available has been increased. There is also now a credit for self-supporting workers between the ages of 25 and 64 with no children.

15.40 Household Employees

Employers of household employees must secure an identification number and must file Schedule H.

15.41 Electronic Filing

Almost all individual returns can now be electronically filed, whether they show a refund or a balance due. It neither increases nor decreases the chance of an audit. One must take or send his return to a transmitter. One must sign Form 8453. The transmitter will mail to the Internal Revenue Service the signature, the W-2 forms, and other necessary materials.

15.42 Social Security Benefits for Nonresident Aliens are now Increased

Also the withholding tax for nonresident aliens at source of income is 30%.

15.43 State Tuition Programs

Contributions are not tax deductible, but earnings are tax deferred. Distributions are taxable to the child in the year of distribution by the amount that they exceed the contribution. These tax benefits now include savings for future college room and board as well as for tuition and fees.

15.44 Death Benefit Exclusion Repealed

The employer of a deceased employee can no longer exclude $5,000 from his income for any death benefits he pays the employee's survivors.

15.45 Personal Injury Damages

Most of these are now taxable, but there are still a few exceptions.

15.46 Employer-Provided Education

There is a $5,250 exclusion for employers who provide education for their employees. But this does not include graduate education.

15.47 Contributions of Stock to Private Foundations

These rules have been re-enacted. Contributors can deduct the fair market value of donated stock.

15.48 Work Opportunity Credit Replaces Targeted Jobs Credit

Employers may deduct 35% of the first $6,000 wages paid to employees hired from targeted groups.

15.49 FUTA Tax

Employers of agricultural aliens need pay no Federal Unemployment tax.

Review Questions

1. *What is inflation?*

   Inflation is the rise in prices of goods and services.

2. *What are inflation adjustments?*

   Inflation adjustments are the revisions in the dollar amounts and percentages that Congress makes in the income tax laws because the dollar is not stable.

3. *What are some of the areas in which Congress makes inflation adjustments?*

   In exemption amounts, standard deductions, itemized deductions, depreciation limits of business-use vehicles, standard mileage allowance for business-use vehicles, rules for earned interest credit.

4. *If we give stock to charity, and this stock has increased in value since we purchased it, how do we value this stock when we deduct it as a charitable contribution on our tax return?*

   We deduct it at fair market value, not at cost.

5. *When we receive an annuity, is it taxable?*

   Usually only the part that represents interest income is taxable. The part that represents initial contribution is really return of capital and thus not taxable.

6. *How do we determine the non-taxable portion of an annuity?*

   Divide the cost of the entire contract by the total number of periodic payments one expects to receive.

7. *If a person is to receive an annuity for the duration of his or her life, how does one determine the non-taxable portion of this annuity?*

   The Internal Revenue Service has an actuarial table that will show the number of payments to be used in the calculation. Then divide the cost of the entire contract by this number.

8. *What is the Kiddie Tax?*

   It is a tax on children under age 14 who have unearned incomes such as interest income and dividend income.

9. *What is the Alternative Minimum Tax?*

   It is a tax placed on people with larger incomes to make sure that they pay at least some tax. In the past, some wealthier people with high incomes have paid no tax at all because of using exclusions, deductions, and credits.

10. *Do people have to pay taxes on their social security benefits?*

    Yes, wealthier recipients have to pay tax on part of their social security benefits.

11. *Why does Congress continue to revise the Income Tax Law?*

    Special interest groups want their taxes lowered. Also, Congress wishes to plug loopholes previously unforeseen by earlier tax writers. Besides this, inflation continues to lower the value of the dollar.

12. *What has happened to the deduction for personal interest payments?*

    These are no longer deductible.

13. Are the costs of facelifts deductible as medical expenses?

Not any longer.

14. If we borrow money to invest in stocks, is the interest on this money tax deductible?

Only to the extent of investment income.

15. What is passive income?

Passive income is income that one earns with little or no work, such as interest income or dividend income.

16. Are passive losses deductible?

Passive losses are deductible only to the extent of passive income.

17. Do sole proprietors, farmers, and landlords deduct tax preparation fees directly from income or on Schedule A?

They can now deduct these fees directly from income.

18. Is it better to make deductions directly from income or via Schedule A?

One saves money if one can legally deduct directly from income.

19. What is the purpose of Schedule C?

Schedule C shows income and expenses of businesses.

20. Should a taxpayer use Schedule C or Schedule C-EZ?

This depends on how complicated a business it is. Usually small business people can use Schedule C-EZ, which is easier.

21. Why do new tax tables go clear to $100,000 taxable income?

This is an adjustment due to inflation.

22. *Why do revised withholding tables for employers go clear to $100,000?*

This is an adjustment due to inflation.

23. *Which is better, an exclusion or a deduction?*

An exclusion is better; this does not have to be reported as income at all.

24. *What types of people are included in Work Targeted Groups?*

Needy families with children, ex-felons, high-risk youth, veterans, people in vocational rehabilitation, summer youth employees, people on supplemental social security income.

25. *How does the Government encourage taxpayers to build more low-income housing?*

By giving people a Low-Income Housing Credit for constructing or rehabilitating low-income housing.

26. *The government rules now allow businesses to amortize Goodwill and Going-Concern Value over a shorter period than previously. How does this affect taxpayers?*

It cuts down their net income and thus lowers their taxes during the years of write-off.

27. *How do new "Safe-Harbor" rules for people paying estimated taxes affect such taxpayers?*

It gives them a clearer idea of how much estimated taxes they need to pay in order to avoid penalties for underpayment.

28. *If tipped employees sign and follow the Tipped Employees Participation Agreement, how does it help them?*

It usually keeps them from being audited by the Internal Revenue Service.

29. *Why is Debt Discharge taxable?*

Taxpayers are relieved by creditors from having to pay their debts. The Government considers this as income and therefore taxes it.

30. *On the income tax form the taxpayer may designate $3 to the Presidential Election Campaign Fund. How does this affect the taxpayer's liability?*

It doesn't affect it.

31. *How has Congress moved in recent years to help taxpayers?*

It has voted "Safe Harbors" for people underpaying their estimated taxes. It has also shifted the "Burden of Proof" to the Internal Revenue Services in court cases. Previously this "Burden of Proof" had been on the shoulders of the taxpayers.

32. *How has the law helped employers of agricultural aliens?*

These employers no longer have to pay the Federal Unemployment Tax.

33. *If one suffers a passive loss, is it deductible for income tax purposes?*

Only to the extent that it can be deductible from passive gains.

34. *Have Moving Expense requirements recently become easier or more stringent for the taxpayer?*

More stringent.

35. *Why do elderly higher-income taxpayers complain of so-called double taxation on their social security benefits?*

They originally were required to pay for their social security through the Federal Insurance Contributions Act (FICA), and now at old age they must again pay income tax on a portion of their Social Security benefits.

36. *How does the Government encourage business investment in poverty-stricken areas?*

By setting up "Empowerment Zones" wherein businesses that invest there get faster depreciation rates and also can get credits on their alternative minimum taxes.

37. *How do federal tax laws aid people on Indian Reservations?*

Taxpayers who set up businesses on Indian Reservations are allowed to depreciate assets at a faster rate than they would otherwise. They also get a tax credit for hiring tribal members whose wages do not exceed $30,000.

38. *How do the federal tax laws encourage self-employed people to buy health insurance?*

These taxpayers are now allowed a deduction of 30% of their health insurance costs.

39. *What is the purpose of the Earned Income Credit?*

To help low-income taxpayers.

40. *Can military people apply for the Earned Income Credit?*

Yes.

41. *Can prisoners apply for the Earned Income Credit?*

No.

42. *Can non-resident aliens apply for the Earned Income Credit?*

No.

43. *Can self-supporting workers with no children receive the Earned Income Credit?*

Yes.

44. *If a taxpayer hires a household employee, should the taxpayer secure an identification number?*

Yes.

45. *If a taxpayer hires a household employee, how should he reveal this on his income tax?*

By filing a Schedule H.

46. *If a taxpayer files electronically, will this increase the chance of an audit?*

No.

47. *If a taxpayer files electronically, will this do away with any paperwork to be mailed to the Internal Revenue Service?*

No. The transmitter will still have to send in the taxpayer's signature, his W-2 forms, and other papers.

48. *Are contributions to state tuition programs tax deductible?*

No.

49. *Is interest earned on contributions to state tuition programs taxable each year?*

No. They are tax-deferred. Distributions are taxable to the child in the year of distribution to the extent that they exceed the contribution.

50. *Does an employer get an exclusion for providing graduate education to his employee?*

No.

51. *If a taxpayer contributes his stock to a Private Foundation, can he deduct the fair market value of the stock, or must he deduct only the amount that he paid for the stock?*

He may deduct the fair market value of the stock.

52. *Formerly there was a Targeted Jobs Credit. What has replaced this?*

The Work Opportunity Credit.

CHAPTER 16

MORE RECENT CHANGES

16.1 Section 179 Deductions

Air conditioning and heating units are no longer deductible as a Section 179 deduction.

16.2 New Holding Period

The holding period for long-term capital gains has been raised to 18 months from 12 months. (This means that owners of stocks and bonds must hold them for at least 18 months in order to get long-term capital gain benefit.)

16.3 Rules for Gain on Sale of Main Home

Joint filers may now exclude a $500,000 gain on the sale of their main home. Single filers may exclude $250,000. Also, this exclusion may be made every two years.

16.4 Adoption Credit

A $5000 credit may be claimed for each child whom the filers adopt. There are even more liberal credits for parents adopting children with special needs.

16.5 Long-Term Health Care Insurance

Premiums paid for this type of insurance are deductible as a medical expense. Benefits received from insurance companies by taxpayer are excludable from income.

16.6 Retirement Changes

(a) The 15% tax on Excess Retirement Distributions from Individual Retirement Accounts and qualified retirement plans has now been eliminated.

(b) Older employees must start taking required retirement distributions either at age 70 1/2 or they may wait until they retire, if it is after that age.

(c) Simple Retirement Plans and 401(k) Plans. Rules for these plans have been set up by the Internal Revenue Service for self-employed people and for employers and employees in firms hiring 100 or fewer people.

16.7 Medical Savings Accounts

Rules for setting up these accounts are experimental and limited to 750,000 people during these first years. They are designed to provide affordable health coverage. These accounts now are only for employees of firms with 50 or fewer employees, or for the self-employed. Contributions to the plan help one pay the deductible amount if the need arises. Contributions are tax deductible.

16.8 Accelerated Death Benefits

Life insurance proceeds paid by the life insurance company to chronically ill or terminally ill beneficiaries are excluded from the income of these beneficiaries up to $175 per day.

16.9 Section 179 Expense Deduction

Fast first-year depreciation of business assets could be deducted up to $18,000 in 1997 and this figure is gradually raised to $25,000 in 2003.

16.10 Health Insurance for Self-Employed People

These people may deduct, as an adjustment to income, 50% of the cost of their health insurance. This gradually increases to 100% in the year 2007.

16.11 Cancellation (Forgiveness) of Student Loans

These are no longer taxable if the following conditions are all met:

(a) The student was or is attending a tax-exempt institution.

(b) The student was not, or is not an employee of the institution.

(c) After graduation the student is required to work for a time in a profession or geographic area.

(d) The graduate is fulfilling a public service requirement.

16.12 Orphan Drug Credit

This is a permanent credit for clinical testing of drugs for treatment of rare diseases.

16.13 Public Officers Killed in the Line of Duty

Their survivors' pensions are excludable from gross income. This would include survivors of police, fire fighters, rescue workers, and ambulance crews.

16.14 Sale of Livestock Due to Weather-Related Conditions

If the farmer or rancher uses the cash method of accounting, and if this takes place in a federally designated area, the proceeds of any sales above the amount of ordinary sales may be deferred until the year after the year of sale.

16.15 Clean Fuel Vehicles Deduction

This can be taken only in the first year of use. It is for modified vehicles using only clean-burning fuel. The depreciation can be taken only on the cost of vehicle before modifications. The taxpayer must be the original user of the vehicle. The deduction is $2,000 for car or small truck; $5,000 for medium-sized truck or for a van; and $50,000 for large truck or a bus.

16.16 Credit for Washington, D.C., First-Time Home Buyers

This is a $5,000 credit for taxpayers buying under these conditions who have a Modified Adjusted Gross Income of under $70,000. The credit is gradually phased out at higher levels.

16.17 Burden of Proof

In court cases the Government now has the burden of proof, as long as the taxpayer can substantiate his figures, keeps records, and cooperates reasonably.

16.18 Innocent Spouse

This person now can use a tax return based on his or her sole income as if he or she were married and filing separately.

16.19 Disabled Taxpayers

The Statue of Limitations will now be suspended for a disabled taxpayer claiming a refund, as long as it has been medically determined that the person has a mental or physical disability preventing him from managing his personal affairs, and that this disability may result in death or that it will last 12 months or more. This will allow the taxpayer more time to claim any possible refunds.

16.20 Denial of Refund

If the Internal Revenue Service denies the taxpayer a refund, it must now inform him or her of its reasoning for doing so.

16.21 Third-Party Contacts

If the Internal Revenue Service contacts others in an attempt to collect taxes from a taxpayer, it must inform the taxpayer. There are a few exceptions to this new rule.

16.22 No Financial Status Audit

From now on, the Internal Revenue Service cannot usually determine the client's financial status unless there is a reasonable indication of unreported income.

16.23 Selection for an Audit

The Internal Revenue Service must simply express the procedure that it uses in determining whether or not a taxpayer will be audited.

16.24 Privileged Communications

These are private conversations between a taxpayer and certain professionals that do not have to be divulged to the Internal Revenue Service. These professionals include lawyers, enrolled agents, and enrolled actuaries. However, these communications are privileged only in noncriminal matters.

16.25 Interest Paid and Charged

From now on, the interest rate that the Government pays to tax overpayers must equal the interest rate that the Government charges underpayers.

16.26 Disaster Areas

In government declared disaster areas there will be no interest on owed taxes for the length of time of the disaster extensions.

16.27 Interest and Penalties

The interest on and penalties for unpaid taxes are suspended if the Internal Revenue Service has not notified the taxpayer that he owes an additional tax within 18 months of the original date of the return or the date of filing.

16.28 Collections

The Internal Revenue Service must inform the taxpayer if it intends to collect his taxes by levy or by seizure. The Internal Revenue Service will not be allowed to seize certain furniture, personal items, worktools, and books. The Internal Revenue Service cannot seize the taxpayer's personal residence in order to satisfy debts of $500 or less.

16.29 Offers of Compromise

The Internal Revenue Service must usually compromise in collecting from low-income taxpayers.

16.30 Debt Collection Practices

The Internal Revenue Service must not harass the debtor. They can phone debtors only between the hours of 8 a.m. and 9 p.m.

16.31 Capital Gains

The rate is now 20% for gains on the sale of assets owned more than 18 months.

16.32 Child Tax Credit

This is now $500 credit for each qualifying child.

16.33 Hope Credit

This is a credit for up to $1,500 for first-year and sophomore college students' tuition and fees. It is for the taxpayer himself (herself) or for the taxpayer's spouse or dependent.

16.34 Lifetime Learning Credit

This is a 20% credit for the first $5,000 for tuition and fees for the taxpayer himself (herself), or the taxpayer's spouse or dependent. This credit could be for senior college as well as for junior college.

16.35 Education Individual Retirement Accounts

These are savings plans for a child's future college education. They allow a $500 nondeductible contribution per beneficiary per year. Earnings grow tax free; and withdrawals for educational purposes are tax free.

16.36 Deduction for Student Loan Interest

Interest on loans used for higher-education expenses for self, spouse, or dependent is deductible before determining adjusted gross income for the first 60 months in which interest is required. However, there are certain top limits.

16.37 Roth Individual Retirement Accounts

A taxpayer may make annual nondeductible contributions to this I.R.A. up to $2,000 or his earned income, whichever is greater. Earnings grow tax free. Distributions are also tax free.

16.38 Penalty-Free I.R.A. Distributions

No Individual Retirement Account withdrawals will be subject to the usual 10% penalty if they are used for higher education or for first-time home buyer expense up to $10,000.

16.39 Employer-Sponsored Retirement Plans

The new rules allow higher phaseout thresholds for spouses.

16.40 Net Operating Losses

Taxpayers with net operating losses are allowed to refigure taxes for previous years (carrybacks). The new regulations cut the carrybacks from 3 years to 2 years. Then they are also allowed to deduct any more net operating losses from income of future years. These are called carryforwards. The new provisions allow the carryforward period to be increased to 20 years instead of 15 years as was previously allowed.

16.41 Welfare to Work Credit

Employers of people previously on welfare are allowed a credit equal to 35% of the first $10,000 salary in the employee's first year on the job, and 50% of the employee's first $10,000 in his second year on the job.

16.42 Increased Meal Deduction for Transportation Workers

These are for such workers as bus drivers, truck drivers, or railroad workers. Deductions for meals while away from home are gradually increased from 50% to 80% if these workers are subject to Department of Transportation hours-of-service limitations.

16.43 Income Averaging for Farmers

Farmers may now average their incomes over a 3-year period if they wish, in order legally to cut down on their income tax.

16.44 Adjusted Gross Income for Earned Income Credit Purposes

Taxpayers wishing to claim the Earned Income Credit must add in their tax-exempt interest, and the nontaxable distributions from pensions, annuities, and Individual Retirement Accounts in computing their Adjusted Gross Income for Earned Income Credit purposes.

16.45 Foreign Earned Income Exclusion

Taxpayers earning income in foreign countries have an exclusion from U.S. taxes since they are usually taxed on this income in the foreign country. Under the new rules this exclusion gradually rises from $70,000 to $80,000.

16.46 Increased Standard Deduction for Dependents

The dependent's standard deduction now becomes the smaller of $700 or the dependent's earned income plus $250.

16.47 Rural Mail Carriers

These people can now deduct on their income taxes only the rate of reimbursement that the Postal Service allows them.

16.48 Home Office Deduction

Taxpayers may now take a home office deduction as long as this office is used regularly and exclusively for business.

Review Questions

1. *How have the new tax laws helped people with long-term capital gains?*

    These people need only pay 20% tax on these gains.

2. *Have the new rules for Gain on Sale of Main Home helped or hindered taxpayers?*

    They have helped taxpayers greatly. Now very few people will have to pay taxes on these gains.

3. *How have the recent tax-law changes helped taxpayers who adopt children?*

    They get a $5000 tax credit for each child they adopt.

4. *How have the recent tax-law changes helped people who buy long-term health care insurance?*

    Premiums are deductible as a medical expense. Benefits are excludable from income.

5. *What has happened to the 15% tax on Excess Retirement Distributions from Individual Retirement Accounts?*

    This tax has been eliminated.

6. *How have older employees benefited from recent tax-law changes?*

    If they wish to retire at a time later than the date on which they reach age 70 1/2, they don't need to start taking the formerly required I.R.A. distributions until the date on which they finally retire.

7. *How do recent tax-law changes help employees of small firms?*

    They encourage employers in these small firms to set up Simple Retirement Plans and 401(k) Plans by making the plans easier to execute and also tax deferred.

8. *What is the purpose of Medical Savings Accounts?*

   To provide affordable health coverage.

9. *How have recent tax-law changes helped the chronically ill and dying taxpayers?*

   Their accelerated death benefits are now excluded from income.

10. *How have recent tax-law changes helped businesses with their depreciation problems?*

    Businesses buying non-land assets termed Section 179 Assets were able to deduct the first $18,000 as a business expense the first year. This is gradually being raised to $25,000.

11. *What type of student loans are no longer taxable when forgiven?*

    Cancellation or forgiveness of these loans is no longer taxable if the student was attending a tax-exempt institution, if the student was not an employee of the institution, and if after graduation the student was required to work for a time in a profession or in a certain geographic area, and if the graduate is fulfilling a public service requirement.

12. *What is the Orphan Drug Credit?*

    It's a tax credit to be taken by taxpayers doing clinical testing of drugs for the treatment of rare diseases.

13. *What benefit do the recent tax-law changes give to beneficiaries of police officers, fire fighters, rescue workers, and ambulance crews killed in the line of duty?*

    The survivors' pensions are excludable from income for income tax purposes.

14. *What benefits are given to farmers and ranchers wishing to sell livestock prematurely due to severe weather conditions?*

    If they are in a federally-designated area, any proceeds from sale of livestock above ordinary sales may be deferred a year.

15. *How can a taxpayer who modifies his vehicle to burn only clean-burning fuel be helped by recent tax-law changes?*

He can get a clean-fuel deduction.

16. *How can first-time home buyers in Washington, D.C., be helped by recent changes in the income tax laws?*

They get a $5,000 tax credit, but their modified adjusted gross income must be under $70,000. It is phased out at higher income levels.

17. *How do recent tax-law changes help innocent spouses?*

These spouses may now file a tax return on their income only as if they were married and filing separately.

18. *How are disabled taxpayers aided by recent changes in the income-tax laws?*

They will have longer periods of time to claim possible refunds.

19. *How are taxpayers protected by recent changes in the tax law?*

IRS must now inform taxpayers of its reasons for denying them refunds. IRS also must usually inform a taxpayer if it is contacting others in an attempt to collect taxes from the taxpayer. From now on, the IRS cannot usually determine the client's financial status in making collections. The IRS must tell the taxpayer the procedure it used to determine whether or not the taxpayer will be audited.

20. *How does the new law protect the taxpayer's privileged communications?*

Private conversations between the taxpayer and his lawyer, or his enrolled agent, or his enrolled actuary need not be divulged to the Internal Revenue Service as long as it is not a criminal case.

21. *How do the recent laws affect interest rates that the IRS charges taxpayers?*

Interest rates that the government charges underpayers must be the same as the rates that the government pays to overpayers.

22. *How do recent tax-law changes affect people living in federally-declared disaster areas?*

No interest will be assessed on owed taxes for the length of time of the disaster extensions.

23. *How do recent tax-law changes protect taxpayers from tardy claims of the Internal Revenue Service?*

Interest and penalties on unpaid taxes are suspended if the IRS waits until after 18 months of the return's date before notifying the taxpayer of these charges.

24. *How have recent tax-law changes affected the method by which the Internal Revenue Service can collect from the taxpayer?*

The IRS must inform the taxpayer whether it will collect by levy or by seizure. The IRS will no longer be allowed to seize certain of the taxpayer's furniture, personal items, worktools, or books. The IRS will no longer be allowed to seize the taxpayer's personal residence to satisfy debts of $500 or less.

25. *How do recent tax-law changes protect low-income taxpayers?*

The Internal Revenue Service must now usually offer to compromise.

26. *How do recent tax-law changes prevent harassment of taxpayers?*

The IRS can no longer phone taxpayers prior to 8 a.m. or later than 9 p.m.

27. *What is the Hope Credit?*

This cuts the taxes of the taxpayer or his spouse or dependent by up to $1,500 to pay for a junior college student's tuition and fees.

28. *What is the Lifetime Learning Credit?*

This is a 20% credit for the first $5,000 for tuition and fees for a taxpayer sending himself or spouse or dependent to college. It can include senior college as well as junior college.

29. *What are the tax implications of Education Individual Retirement Accounts?*

They allow a $500 nondeductible contribution per beneficiary per year. Earnings grow tax free, and withdrawals for educational purposes are tax free.

30. *Is interest that students pay on their student loans deductible for income tax purposes?*

Yes, if these are for higher education for taxpayer, his spouse, or his dependent. This is deductible from adjusted gross income for the first 60 months in which interest is required.

31. *What are the main features of a Roth Individual Retirement Account?*

A taxpayer makes up to $2000 annual nondeductible contribution to this I.R.A. If his earnings are less than $2000, he may contribute all his earnings if he wishes. Earnings grow tax free, and distributions are also tax free.

32. *Why are there penalties on some Individual Retirement Accounts?*

Penalties have been 10% for early withdrawals prior to age 59 1/2. This is to encourage taxpayers to keep their money in these accounts until almost retirement age.

33. *How have these early withdrawal penalties on I.R.A.'s been changed by recent tax laws?*

Early withdrawals from I.R.A.'s will no longer be penalized if the money is used for higher education or for first-time home buying expense up to $10,000.

34. *What is the purpose of Work-to-Welfare Credit?*

   This encourages prospective employers to hire welfare recipients.

35. *How are some transportation workers favored by recent income-tax law changes?*

   Deductions for meals while away from home are gradually over the years increasing from 50% to 80% if these workers are subject to Department of Transportation hours-of-service limitations.

36. *How are farmers aided by recent changes in the income tax laws?*

   Farmers may now average their incomes over a 3-year period. Farmers should figure their tax both ways to determine which method (the regular method or the 3-year income-averaging method) will result in lower taxes for them.

37. *How are taxpayers earning incomes in foreign countries now helped by recent changes in the income tax law?*

   Their Foreign Earned Income Exclusion over the years will gradually rise from $70,000 to $80,000.

38. *How are rural mail carriers affected by changes in the income tax laws?*

   These carriers no longer have special income tax rules. They are from now on allowed to deduct only the rate of reimbursement that the Postal Service allows them.

39. *How have Home Office Deductions improved under recent laws?*

   Taxpayers may make these deductions as long as their home office section of the house is used exclusively and regularly for business.

MARQUIS
Marquis Book Printing Inc.

Québec, Canada
2010